THE LAST WHITE CLASS

THE LAST WHITE CLASS

by

marge piercy
and ira wood

a play about neighborhood terror

✳ the crossing press/trumansburg, new york 14886

cover and book design: Mary A. Scott
back cover photograph: Robert M. Shapiro

Library of Congress Cataloging in Publication Data
Piercy, Marge
        The last white class.

        I. Wood, Ira, joint author. II. Title.
PS3566.I413   812'.5'4   79-18884
ISBN 0-89594-028-0
ISBN 0-89594-027-2 pbk.

foreword

We extend grateful acknowledgement for the help of a great many people.

First of all, the idea for a play about bussing in Boston originated with Gene Bruskin and Ira Wood; they wrote a draft for a two-act play with music. That script was rewritten by Susan Eisenberg and Ira Wood and partially improvised by the Harpers Ferry Theater Group (at varying times including Gene Bruskin, DuQuincy Cooks, Susan Eisenberg, Laura Foner, Cathy Frazier, Mark Frazier, Meredith Rogers, Dana Stancil, Victor Teixeira, Alphonda Thorn, Ira Wood, Evangeline Young) under the direction of Susan Eisenberg. In that form a two-act 50-minute play *It's Not the Bus* was performed three times at St. Johns, St. James Church in Roxbury in mid-December, 1976. After those performances, the group decided to dissolve, divide up their resources and abandon the project.

From the short play mentioned above, we have taken over the basic idea of a Black family under attack in a white neighborhood during the introduction of bussing, and the commitment to a play that might be useful in combatting racism.

It is difficult to acknowledge all of the individual and collective contributions that so many people made to the previous attempts at producing a play about racism, albeit

very different plays from this play. We are grateful to
everyone who gave time, energy, ideas, research and
encouragement to this long project. However, we alone must
bear responsibility for the characters, the language, the
concept and the politics of *The Last White Class*.

Partially we wrote this play because we wanted to work
together. Partially we wrote this play because we both felt a
strong need for something like it politically. We both feel
Boston is an important city in which to examine what's
going on in the North. Boston has one of the smallest
percentages of non-white people of any of the large Eastern
cities; Boston is the scene of one of the most publicized
battles among working people for the limited jobs, the lacking
city services, the decaying neighborhoods, the right to equal
treatment in an archaic school system.

When *It's Not the Bus* was abandoned, we two
abandoned our previous intention to work on a comedy
about sex roles, and decided we could not let the
commitment to write a play on racism die with the previous
play. We found it maddening to learn to work together and
hard to begin again and make a play that was not in place of
previous attempts, but something new. It had to be a play
that would reflect both our differing and not always
overlapping political passions and experiences and concerns.
We alone must bear responsibility for what we have wrought
out of all this promise and turmoil. We were determined
that a play should finally happen, and we have struggled with
each other as fiercely as with any enemy to make it come at
last to the light.

Marge Piercy
Ira Wood

cast of characters

(In the order of their appearance)

PETER THIBAULT, white, 29, bartender at the Jack of Diamonds.

MICHAEL THIBAULT, white, 18, his younger brother.

TERRY BURKE, white, 17, MICHAEL's friend, still in high school.

FRANKLIN DOUGLAS, Black, 19, in cooking school.

SUZANNE DOUGLAS, Black, 16, his sister, in the same high school as TERRY.

ROSETTA DOUGLAS, Black, 38, their mother, a widow, works in a fabric store.

CURTIS McDONALD, Black, 33, a carpenter.

EILEEN BURKE, white, 39, TERRY's mother, has recently gone back to work in an office.

JOE BURKE, white, 42, TERRY's father, unemployed for 14 months.

GINA CASEY, white, 29, mother of two small children, works as a dental assistant.

KEITH CASEY, white, 30, her husband, JOE's cousin on his mother's side. Accountant of the Casey Hardware Store.

MRS. ROSS (PAULINE), white, 56, director of the Little City Hall.

TIME: Four days in Mid-April, 1975, the spring of Boston's first school year under court-ordered bussing.

PLACE: A neighborhood in the Dorchester section of Boston.

Note on Time and Place: We feel the play can be adapted to a similar situation in any large Northern city in the United States.

synopsis of scenes

AUTHORS' NOTES ON THE SETTING

Six homes are represented in the play, as well as a bar, a
Little City Hall, and the outside of abandoned storefronts.
The setting can be as elaborate or as simple as taste and
finances dictate. The most important feeling to achieve is that
of neighborhood life.

The DOUGLAS family living room with its porch and
partial view of the kitchen could be at CENTER to the RIGHT.
The BURKE family kitchen with its view of living room and
bedroom could be at CENTER to the LEFT. A short scene in
CURTIS' bedroom occurs in another neighborhood and
should be played with all else dark. DOWN is the bar and the
Little City Hall. DOWN CENTER is the street.

The play could also be staged with minimal construction.
A few carefully chosen props would indicate whose living
room, whose kitchen, whose bedroom we are looking at.

ACT 1

scene 1

The stage represents a working-class neighborhood of frame houses, built about seventy-five years ago. The sky is low, the neighborhood is aging, most things are the color of smoke. Nothing in these old houses is quite horizontal or perpendicular but settled a little awry. The houses press together, and the lives inside are close. In many of the houses two or three generations still live, sometimes each to a flat or floor-through. Both the BURKES and the DOUGLASES, however, inhabit single family dwellings on the same block. Although this is an inner city neighborhood with services and schools decaying fast, many of the people who live here were born in these blocks.

FRANKLIN DOUGLAS sits in his living room listening to the radio as he does his homework. Top forty tunes of spring 1975 are heard. Noise in his backyard brings him to his door. As he opens it, calling out, two white youths run past him and down the block, one carrying a spray can of red paint. The lights dim.

The lights come up on PETER THIBAULT's living room.

It is a Wednesday in mid-April, just after noon in PETER THIBAULT's bachelor apartment. Above the couch is a black velvet irridescent picture of sex and conquest (one of those pictures that abound in large furniture stores: a woman with huge breasts and torn clothing about to be eaten by a hungry lion). The apartment is neat and hardly used; mostly PETER just sleeps here. The light is high noon through drawn draperies. On the coffee table is a container of orange juice. Posters rest against the end of the couch. Four words are visible to the audience: SAVE OUR CHILDREN and RALLY, plus the name IRIS MAYO

TEAGUE. There is a kitchen in back of this room, unseen.

PETER is partly dressed, having just woken up. He sits on the couch.

A buzzer sounds as PETER is reading the newspaper.

PETER

(Loudly.) Come on in, I left it open.

MICHAEL

(Enters carrying a full bag of laundry and a small paper bag, both in one hand. His other hand is in his pocket. Visible on his tan leather jacket is a streak of red spray paint. MICHAEL is taller than PETER and overweight.)

Brought your laundry. Mom says you should call her.

(Looks at the posters, circles the table. Sits on the other chair and opens the bag. Takes out a large tuna sub. PETER watches, disapproving. MICHAEL takes a long swig from the orange juice container.)

PETER

Could you get a glass?

MICHAEL

There aren't any.

PETER

In the kitchen.

MICHAEL

You drink out of the carton.

PETER

Yeah, but it's my carton. You want some, get a glass.

> *(MICHAEL sullen. Doesn't get a glass).*

How did it go?

MICHAEL

(Enjoys it.) Beautiful!

PETER

Anybody see you?

MICHAEL

Yeah, but he didn't catch us. Stupid nigger chased us halfway up the block, but he didn't even get close.

PETER

He recognize you?

MICHAEL

No man, it was beautiful. He didn't even see us till we were practically done ... Got a cigarette?

PETER

Smoke in front of Dad these days?

> *(Gives him one. Getting at something.)*

So nobody saw you?

MICHAEL

I told you ... nobody. It was beautiful. We did just like you said.

PETER

(Begins to pace. Becomes an interrogator.) So it's beautiful, beautiful ... Where did you get that sub?

MICHAEL

What's the matter, I didn't eat nothing all day.

PETER

Where did you get it? Joey's?

MICHAEL

Yeah, Joey's. I always get it at Joey's.

PETER

Who sold it to you?

MICHAEL

The guy ... What're you crazy or something? I'm telling you, nobody saw us.

PETER

Look at your jacket.

MICHAEL

(Sees his jacket sleeve is covered on the underside with red paint.) Who's gonna know what it's from?

PETER

(Slowly.) You walked into the corner grocery dripping with red paint. Then you came straight here.

> *(MICHAEL doesn't answer.)*

(Demands an answer.) Right?

MICHAEL

It could be from anything.

PETER

(Calm.) Michael. You did a good thing today. Real good. But you got to be more careful ...

> *(Goes up to MICHAEL, puts his arm around him. MICHAEL*

> *freezes. He squeezes MICHAEL's neck.)*

Do you hear me?

MICHAEL
(Squeals, wriggles free.) Aw, Peter ...

PETER
(As he walks into the back room his tone is less hostile.) Who was with you?

> *(Comes out with a knife and two glasses. Cuts the sub, pours two glasses of juice. Sits back on the couch and eats his section of the sub.)*

MICHAEL
Vincent Drago. A kid from school.

PETER
That's it? One kid?

MICHAEL
(Defensive.) I got a lot of guys.

PETER
Good. We're gonna need guys we can trust. Guys who'll do what you say.

MICHAEL
Why should they do what I say.

PETER
'Cause they're stupid.

MICHAEL
(Hurt.) Shut up.

PETER

You find a thing somebody needs and you help. You don't
say, 'Here, man, I'll give you a car.' You tell them you know
a guy who can get them a good deal. When somebody needs
a job, they're in some trouble, we can put in a good word for
them.

MICHAEL

Me? ... What do we have to do?

PETER

Find guys who are pissed off. Yours was the last white class
at the school, man, these kids don't know how it was. Girls
weren't scared to walk in the halls. All white guys were on
the teams. Everybody got a job when they came out ... I
want you to get guys who want to see things like they were
and who aren't scared to fight.

MICHAEL

Maybe we could have like a club. You think we could have
jackets? The guys would dig that.

PETER

(Pleased.) Sounds good. You bring the guys together ... I
got a lot of these posters still to go up.

MICHAEL

I already been all over the neighborhood. How come we're
working for **her**?

PETER

They got to be up by tonight — Rally's Sunday. Iris is gonna
win. You work for the winners and you become a winner,
just like you're working for me. Sculley hates her guts but
politics is politics.

MICHAEL

(Takes out a Ring Ding.) All those posters?

PETER

You had lunch. What are you eating that garbage for?

MICHAEL

Get off my back.

PETER

You're getting as fat as a pig.

MICHAEL

Leave me alone. I'm not fat. I'm big. It's muscle.
(Flexes.)

PETER

There's muscle in that big ass of yours?

MICHAEL

(As he leaves with the posters.) Shut up.

◆ ◆ ◆

scene 2

The front of a vacant store. With a bucket of wheat paste and a brush, MICHAEL puts up posters for the Rally on Sunday.

MICHAEL

(To the posters.) Stupid cow! You got a face like a pizza. VOTE FOR THE WAR HERO'S WIDOW. Probably went **into** the war to get away from you --

TERRY

(Enters. He is a lanky kid of medium height wearing a faded and torn dungaree jacket and jeans. He attempts to be neat, but his clothes are worn thin. Stands and watches MICHAEL for a moment before interrupting) Who are you talking to?

MICHAEL

(Scared. Whips around with brush as if to protect himself.)
Don't come up behind me like that, asshole.

TERRY

What're you doing?

MICHAEL

Getting laid. What's it look like I'm doing. Give me a hand.

> *(Shows him how to brush paste
> on the back and front of a poster.
> TERRY takes a turn and then
> another and another. Soon
> TERRY is doing all the work
> while MICHAEL watches.)*

TERRY

Your brother making you do this?

MICHAEL

He doesn't **make** me do anything. I'm working for him.

TERRY

You getting paid?

MICHAEL

Yeah, I'm getting paid. People who work usually get paid.
Don't they? Except if you're in school, then you work for
nothing ...

> *(Eight posters are up now.
> TERRY stops.)*

TERRY

More?

MICHAEL

Yeah, why not. Gimme the brush.

(Puts up one more and stops.)

I gotta have fifty of these up by tonight ... You hook school
again?

TERRY

(Sits.) Yeah.

MICHAEL

What'd you do?

TERRY

(Bored.) Nothing. Hung around the Commons. Played some
pin ball ... Maybe your brother could hire me to put up
posters?

MICHAEL

Nah, I'm almost done. I been doing it all week.

TERRY

You think your brother could get me a job?

MICHAEL

Sure, if he wanted to. Not if you're in school.

TERRY

If I had a job, my parents wouldn't make me go. Could he
get me a job at the bar? Like one of those bar boys, bringing
ice and glasses. I bet Peter meets a lot of girls working in a
bar.

MICHAEL

He gets laid any time he wants. All he's gotta do is make a
phone call.

TERRY

Who does he call?

MICHAEL

Don't you think I'd call if I knew who? He had a bitch over

there this morning. He says to me, 'Mikey, you want this
bitch?' I says, 'No man, I want a blond.' He says, 'Okay,
come on over tomorrow night.' I says, 'All right.' So
tomorrow night I'm gonna go over and get laid by some
blond bitch.

TERRY
You were at Peter's today. What else happened?

MICHAEL
First he got us subs. As much as we wanted.

(Slowly, tastes each item.)

Tuna, meatball, sausage, everything. And a six pack of beer.
Then we sat down and talked business.

TERRY
Did that girl eat with you? Was she dressed? What business?

MICHAEL
I can't tell you, man. Security.

TERRY
Come on, Michael! What?

MICHAEL
This is serious business. You can't go crying to your mother
like you did when Peter bought us beer --

TERRY
That was in ninth grade.

MICHAEL
Do you know how things used to be around here? A lot
better. Peter says everything started falling apart since the
niggers started coming to our school.

TERRY
What are you getting at?

MICHAEL

What we need around here is a bunch of guys who are leaders -- guys who aint afraid to back up what they believe in. We need an organization.

TERRY

A gang, man?

MICHAEL

It's gonna give people courage. Peter says there's money behind it. People with connections. You need a favor, you get a favor. It's politics, man.

TERRY

And Peter could get me a job?

MICHAEL

And we get jackets. Maybe a van, too, he said. With a C.B. radio.

TERRY

Come on, Michael.

MICHAEL

Talk to him yourself. Go to the bar anytime ..... Hey, look down the street. Check this out.

TERRY

What?

MICHAEL

Coming toward us. Isn't that your neighbor? Miss Suzanne Douglas.

TERRY

So what?

MICHAEL

What do you mean so what? You get any pussy lately? I bet Darlene don't put out no feels for you.

*(SUZANNE DOUGLAS enters
carrying books on her way home
from school. She is an attractive
Black adolescent, moderately tall,
dressed in slacks and blouse. She
wears a jacket, open. As soon as
she sees the two boys, she begins
to move cautiously.)*

TERRY

Shut up, Michael. Your brother wants you to put up these
crappy posters. You gonna put them up or not?

MICHAEL

Let's have some fun. Does she put out?

TERRY

How do I know? I don't know what everybody on my block
does.

MICHAEL

Well, I'd like to know what she does. Ever had any black
pussy, Terry?

TERRY

As much as you've had, asshole.

*(SUZANNE tries to cross the
street but MICHAEL runs to
block her path. Stands in front
of her. She has to stop. TERRY
comes reluctantly behind.)*

MICHAEL

Hi, Suzie. Want to take a ride in my car?

SUZANNE

Get out of my way.

(Clutches her books at her chest.)

TERRY

Michael! Let's go.

MICHAEL

What're you hiding there?

SUZANNE

(Tries to sidestep him, but he's wider and taller and moves with her.) Get away from me.

MICHAEL

We want to see what you got.

TERRY

> *(SUZANNE glares at TERRY.)*

I didn't say that.

MICHAEL

Let me see, honey. Just let me feel those nice black tits.

> *(Tries to pull her clutched arms
> away from her chest.)*

SUZANNE

(Quickly steps back forcing him off balance. Raises her books and smashes him in the belly.) Don't put your filthy hands on me!

> *(Runs down the street.)*

TERRY

(Steps in, distracting MICHAEL as he holds his belly.) What're you trying to do, man?

MICHAEL

(Pushes TERRY aside and chases her, screaming, then stops, clutches his belly again.) Stinking black whore. Run now, we'll get you later.

(To TERRY.)
You see what she did to me?

TERRY
(Whining.) You're gonna get me in trouble, man ... What if she tells my mother?

MICHAEL
(Feeling his belly.)
They're all animals ... I might go to the police.

TERRY
You want me to help you with the rest of these posters or not?

MICHAEL
Sure, if you do good, I'll tell my brother.

TERRY
(He carries out the buckets and the posters. MICHAEL carries the brush as if it were a weapon.) If Peter does get me a job I'm quitting school. No way my parents gonna keep me from getting a job. No way.

(LIGHTS.)

◆ ◆ ◆

scene 3

The home of the DOUGLAS family. The living room is prominent. Off to the right is a porch. In the back is a kitchen, partly seen. In the past the living room received a great deal of attention, which stopped with

*the death of FRANKLIN, SR.
The couch is covered with a well-
worn but beautiful slipcover,
fading where bodies rest, while
the chair has never been covered.
SUZANNE's paintings decorate
the wall, as well as FRANKLIN
JR.'s high school diploma. Two
fancy matching lamps stand on
either side of the couch on old
tables that don't match. A
broken storm window leans
against one of the tables. There
is a dining table with four chairs
near the doorway to the kitchen.*

*Angry and disgusted, FRANKLIN
carries at arm's length piles of
laundry daubed with red paint.
He is a large Black man, the
tallest person in the play. He
throws the laundry down. Goes
out to carry in another armload.
Returns with it.*

SUZANNE

*(Enters. Stands silent for a moment, then throws her books
at the wall. Her legs feel weak with the receding of the
adrenalin flush and she drops in a chair. Sounding
emotionless, almost an announcement.)* Franklin, such a
disgusting thing just happened to me -- Hey!

> *(Seeing the laundry. Leans
> forward, panicked.)*

Is that blood?

FRANKLIN

Red paint. They hit us again. This time the laundry.

(Kicks the pile with his foot.)

You wonder what kind of raggedy-assed perverts get theirs off from taking nice clean laundry and spraying paint all over it.

SUZANNE

They painted our laundry? Our clothes too?

(Gets up, goes to the pile.)

Who did it? Did you see anything this time?

FRANKLIN

Two punks, about an hour and a half ago.

SUZANNE

(Gets down on her knees to rummage through the laundry.)
Coming in the **backyard** in the **daytime** now, it's getting scarier.

FRANKLIN

Didn't seem like they wanted a fight. They ran halfway down the block as soon as they heard the screen door open.

SUZANNE

Look like these sheets have had it. And your jeans. Franklin, look!

*(Holds up the blouse with writing
NIGGERS SUCK on it.)*

My blouse! The only thing I have left from Daddy. Those dumb stupid ... pigs! Franklin, it's not gonna come out!

(She is rubbing at it futilely.)

FRANKLIN

(Paces around her awkwardly.) You don't need a blouse to remember him by. Besides, it was getting small on you.

SUZANNE

It's so sick, Franklin. No way I'm gonna believe our cat
wasn't poisoned now.

(Catching her breath.)

I don't want to go back to that honky school, I don't want to
walk through those streets, I don't want to deal with those
crazy people!

FRANKLIN

Next time we'll act smarter. We'll tote the stuff to the
laundromat again.

(He paces around her.)

Soon as I'm done with school and get me a chef's job, maybe
we'll move out of this damn neighborhood.

SUZANNE

They hate us. They want to kill us like they did Whiskers.

FRANKLIN

What happened to you before?

SUZANNE

(Seals her surface: fixes her clothes, her expression, gets up.)
Two white punks gave me trouble.

FRANKLIN

What did they do? Did they hurt you?

SUZANNE

They tried. You know that kid Terry from up the block? And
that big dumb kid who yells names at us by Joey's Pantry? I
was walking home from school minding my own business when
they started hassling me.

FRANKLIN

It wasn't just street hassling? Guys making cracks.

SUZANNE

(Embarrassed.) They meant business. Grabbing at me. I want Mama to send me over to Aunt Shirley's this summer. I want to meet boys who aren't white punks with murder on their minds. You back me up with Mama.

FRANKLIN

She'll send you if you ask, you know that. We gonna leave her to face this alone?

> *(Looking out the window. He calls her over.)*

Hey, here comes Mama in a car with some dude.

SUZANNE

(Goes to the window beside FRANKLIN.) Don't say nothing to Mama about what happened to me. Nothing really happened, right? She got enough to worry about.

FRANKLIN

She got a right to know.

SUZANNE

No! Franklin, please. She's gonna think I did something wrong ... Keep your mouth shut and I'll take the laundry to the laundromat for you next week.

FRANKLIN

A deal. If it's worth that much to you, all right ... Hmmm. A skinny little dude with fly shoes. What can he want with our Mama?

SUZANNE

Not bad looking. For a must-be middle age man.

> *(ROSETTA and CURTIS enter and walk slowly toward the house side by side. ROSETTA*

carries a bag of groceries.
CURTIS carries a tool box and a
pane of glass.

ROSETTA is dressed for work.
She is lively, especially so now
with the first man she has been
strongly attracted to since her
husband died.

CURTIS, a few years younger, is
coming from a carpenter's job
and is wearing his work clothes.

While ROSETTA and CURTIS
talk outside and then on the
porch, FRANKLIN and
SUZANNE wait quietly for her
to enter the house, sometimes
peeking through the window,
sometimes making inaudible
comments to each other.

ROSETTA

Just a bitty window off to the side. Those dumb crackers
couldn't even hit the picture window. It won't take you no
time at all to stick a new pane in. In the meantime, I'm
gonna fix supper.

CURTIS

That's fine with me. You got a fast worker here.

ROSETTA

I observe that. This here my house. The lawn look mangy
but I put in the daffodils myself.

CURTIS

Suppose I pick a couple for the table? You got any candles?

ROSETTA
Oh, you into saving electricity?

CURTIS
(Sticks one of the flowers behind her ear and one behind his.)
I'm into making electricity with you.

ROSETTA
I think my daughter Suzanne's got some candles. Real pretty ones she made herself in old milk cartons.

CURTIS
You mean she's gonna be home?

ROSETTA
Curtis, honey, both my kids be home. I told you I had two kids.

CURTIS
You want to go out to dinner?

ROSETTA
I want you to see my house and refresh yourself. I'm proud of my house and my kids.

CURTIS
Looks like a solid old house. But I sure would expect you a lonely woman here. Not too many brothers around.

ROSETTA
We was four Black families here but the Johnsons gave up and moved. Lot of Black folks live eight, ten blocks west. But you know I work and I been raising my kids all alone since my husband Franklin die ... Curtis, you ought to seen this place when we moved in. Chickens live in better houses than this one.

CURTIS
That where your fun come from all these years, fixing up your house?

ROSETTA

Whoa, Curtis. I asked you over to fix that window and I
told you I'm gonna make you a real nice dinner. Maybe
you a real fast man, but I'm a real slow woman.

(Joins her arm in his.)

For right now you just come on in and enjoy my
hospitality.

*(Enters the living room, her
arm still in CURTIS'.)*

You two sitting in the living room and no TV on? What
happen, the power fail? I want you to meet a friend of
mine, Curtis McDonald. This here my daughter Suzanne
and my son Franklin.

FRANKLIN

(Comes over. He is taller than CURTIS. Suspicious.) Hi.

CURTIS

*(Surreptitiously, as if scratching his ear, gets the flower out
of his hair.)* Well, you one king size son.

(To ROSETTA.)

You didn't give me the impression you had such **big** children.

FRANKLIN

Mama got married at age three.

ROSETTA

My sweet talking son here, he in cooking school. Tonight
my show but some time you come on over and taste his
homework ...

*(As SUZANNE marches up to
shake his hand.)*

Suzanne the brains of this family ... What got the two of you?
How often do I bring home a guest for dinner? Let's have a
party mood tonight.

SUZANNE

Mama, something awful happened.

FRANKLIN

You better take a look at this.

(As ROSETTA goes over.)

ROSETTA

Paint now! Paint!

(She pokes through the pile.)

Hard working little bastards, they got every damn sheet and
every damn pillowcase. This gonna cost me a week's pay.
The tablecloth too.

SUZANNE

And my blouse! Mama, look.

ROSETTA

(Hugs her.) Oh, baby, I'm sorry. Soon as I can, I'll get you
another just as pretty.

SUZANNE

But it won't be from Daddy.

ROSETTA

I bet our so-called neighbors just hid in their houses pretending
they stone deaf?

CURTIS

How long has this been going on?

ROSETTA

We been living here eight years. After the first six months or
so, we never had any trouble till now. Franklin, you see them
this time?

FRANKLIN

I chased them down the block.

ROSETTA
Guess I better call the police.

> *(Goes to the phone.)*

SUZANNE
When I called up about our cat being poisoned, the police said I should call the Sanitation Department.

FRANKLIN
Mama, remember when I got my job at the Oyster House? They busted me one night just for walking down the street late.

CURTIS
They're both making sense, Rosetta. The police aren't in business to protect Black people.

ROSETTA
What else we gonna do? Aint no Black army gonna camp on our doorstep and protect us.

> *(Dials. FRANKLIN, CURTIS and SUZANNE talk downstage. We hear ROSETTA only when she raises her voice. Otherwise she talks in a murmur.)*

CURTIS
(To FRANKLIN.) Man, you know who these people are been bothering you?

FRANKLIN
I just saw their clothes from behind.

SUZANNE
What were they wearing?

ROSETTA
No! D-O-U-G-L-A-S ... Yes, I've called before! Four times now!

FRANKLIN

One kid had on a tan leather jacket. Checked pants. Other one had on a green army jacket. Farmer jeans.

SUZANNE

The one with the tan jacket, was he big?

(FRANKLIN nods.)

SUZANNE

I know who he is!

CURTIS

(To FRANKLIN.) I think we ought to take a little ride in my car.

ROSETTA

But why do we have to come down in person? ... You said last time you'd send a car, and you never did!

CURTIS

(Continuing.) Find out where those kids hang out. Tell them if they walk anywhere near this house again, they're gonna be crawling away.

(FRANKLIN stands silent.)

ROSETTA

(Hangs up the phone and comes over.) Franklin, we got to go down to the precinct. They say they're gonna send a patrol car around tonight.

SUZANNE

Why, they gonna give those kids a ride up here? Curtis got a better idea.

CURTIS

Rosetta, Franklin and I are going to handle this right now. We're gonna find those punks and put a stop to this.

ROSETTA

I think we'd best let the police handle it.

CURTIS

Bullshit. You believe for one minute they'll stick their necks out for you?

ROSETTA

I been living in this neighborhood for eight years. I own this house. I pay taxes. They may not like it but they damn well have to protect me.

CURTIS

If a Black family don't protect themselves, they in real trouble. Now me and your son gonna take a ride.

ROSETTA

Curtis, no! Franklin got to walk home from the bus alone at night. My daughter got to walk to and from school. I don't want them being targets. I just want the police to handle this. Anybody get hurt, the police done it, not us --

CURTIS

Rosetta, you're being a fool!

ROSETTA

Don't call me a fool in front of my children! You not in Vietnam now. We been living here alone for three years. Don't you go around ordering our affairs!

SUZANNE

Mama, he was trying to help. You were real nice and polite to the cops. How come you get mad at us instead of at them?

ROSETTA

(Takes SUZANNE's face in her hands.) Oh, honey, I'm scared of all the people I love getting hurt ...

(Turns to CURTIS.)

Curtis, I know you trying to help. But just let it be for now. Don't let those sickies ruin our good time along with all my linens. Please sugar?

FRANKLIN

(Moves stiffly.) I'll see what I can do with this used-to-be laundry.

> *(CURTIS stands at the broken window, fingering the glass. SUZANNE follows him over.)*

ROSETTA

Suzanne, do your Mama a big favor. Bring out those fancy candles you made, okay?

> *(SUZANNE stares at her mother and silently leaves.)*

Curtis, I'm gonna start fricaseeing that chicken right now. Forget about the window. Just sit down on the couch and put your feet up.

CURTIS

You got a salty and a sweet side to your tongue, woman. I'll fix the window. But you know, it's just gonna have to be fixed again and again.

◆ ◆ ◆

scene 4

The home of the BURKE family. The kitchen is prominent. Off to the left is a living room, partly seen. The kitchen was once a sunny yellow room, now clean but worn. All the appliances are old. The action centers around a table with four chairs. When the three members of the BURKE family sit together, the vacant chair should be obvious – the chair where Cathy used to sit. On the table is a flowered plastic tablecloth.

TERRY is listening to a baseball game on a transistor radio and miming the actions of a pitcher. EILEEN enters, wearing an old green cloth coat. She carries her purse awkwardly, as the handle is broken. She also carries a box in which a ream of paper originally came, now holding a sizable remnant of cake cut in segments. EILEEN is a short woman with red hair. Her hair is her only remaining vanity, and she touches it for comfort as she talks.

When TERRY turns and sees her, he stops miming immediately and sits at the table.

EILEEN
I'm real glad you're home. I want to talk to you ... Isn't it late for a baseball game?

*(She hangs her coat, picks up
his jacket from a chair and
fingers a new rip in the sleeve.)*

TERRY
*(Obviously caught off guard, he shuts the radio off and starts
to put it away.)* Yeah, but it's the tenth inning and they're
playing in Chicago.

EILEEN
Where did you get the radio?

TERRY
This one? From Michael.

EILEEN
Be careful of it till you give it back. If you shove it around
like that, you could break it.

TERRY
Don't worry. Michael gave it to me.

EILEEN
Michael?

*(Sits at the table and tries to
mend her purse.)*

How come?

TERRY
Somebody left it in the bar ... What am I supposed to do with
the TV broke? We must be the only people in the whole city
who don't even got a TV set.

EILEEN
That's a good set. It just needs fixing. We're extra short since
the unemployment ran out. Soon as your father gets a job –

TERRY

Sure, sure. You can listen to it too, when you're here by yourself ..... Macaroni and cheese again tonight? What's in the box?

EILEEN

We had a little party at work today, and there's some cake left.

(Passes it to him.)

TERRY

(As he opens it.) A birthday party? Wow, chocolate!

EILEEN

Phyllis got laid off from the typing pool, so we had a goodbye party for her and Audrey baked a cake.

(Watches while he gobbles the cake.)

They didn't even give her any warning. She didn't even guess till she found the pink slip in her paycheck.

TERRY

(Mouth full.) Her husband's working, what do you got to worry for?

(Reaches for another piece.)

EILEEN

(Takes it from him.) That's for dessert, Tee. Phyllis has four kids. I wonder what they're going to do about the rest of us, if they're laying people off ...

(She is working herself up to ask something.)

Tee, do you have a lot of homework tonight?

TERRY

Nah.

EILEEN

You're never home at night any more. How do you get your homework done?

(TERRY silent.)

You always used to be truthful with me.

TERRY

I study at Michael's. I like to do my homework with the TV on.

EILEEN

I got a phone call at work today. From your school.

TERRY

Aw.

EILEEN

They said you haven't been there in two weeks. I said, you're wrong, my son leaves for school every morning. Well, he doesn't get here, the man said, the vice principal. He said when the hockey season was done, you started to cut. I felt like such a fool! With you lying to me every day!

TERRY

(Attacks.) I don't want to go to school any more. It's stupid. I want to quit and get a job.

EILEEN

You **have** to finish your education. It's the only chance you got.

TERRY

Mom, it's so boring I can't stand it. They treat you like a prisoner. You got to talk when they tell you, move when they tell you. They can call **you** names and you can't do nothing back or you get suspended.

EILEEN

Maybe it would be better in the college course. I don't know why they didn't put you in there. You used to want to be a teacher.

TERRY

'Cause they don't put kids like me in there.

(Silence.)

If you keep your mouth shut and do everything they tell you, you graduate. So what? The only time the teachers are ever nice to me is right after we win a hockey game.

EILEEN

(Hopefully.) You like hockey.

TERRY

The season's over. And they got colored on the baseball team now. There's always fights in the locker room.

EILEEN

How can you want to drop out now? Your senior year is your best year. I remember the dances, the school's all yours then.

> *(Remembering the most exciting parts of **her** senior year.)*

Pictures and yearbooks and mugs. Remember, Tee, I showed you that snapshot of me on the senior trip --

TERRY

Mom, I never have any money.

EILEEN

But I give you some when I can. Your father'll be working soon.

TERRY

High school's not like it was for you. Now it's lousy with the coloreds they bus in. The last day I went, Mr. Nordella in woodworking told me to make a parson's table for the library with a nigger as my partner.

EILEEN

I don't want to hear that talk in my house! ... Audrey and Lucille are my best friends in the typing pool. Audrey made that cake you were eating ... What's so bad about making a table together? If anybody'd told me before I got this job I'd be telling my life story to a colored woman –

TERRY

Next year they're not just bussing them in here. They're shipping us to Roxbury. So there won't be no senior class for us. Ten years with the same guys and then they bus you out. They're robbing us blind.

EILEEN

That's just rumors.

TERRY

Aw, it's all over school. Michael showed me this.

> *(Pulls out a pamphlet and hands it to her.)*

EILEEN

I'm gonna call Gina, if she's home from work. She'll know ... She goes to all that Parent-Council stuff.

TERRY

Never mind, Peter Thibault's gonna get me and Michael jobs. Michael told me this afternoon.

EILEEN

(With disgust.) Peter Thibault ... Did Michael tell you how Peter got Peggy Dawley in trouble in high school?

                    TERRY
What's that got to do with him giving me a job?

                    EILEEN
Instead of marrying her, he ran off and joined the Army –

                    TERRY
It was the Marines. He was a hero in Vietnam. Don't you
know he got a silver star? You ought to see the medals he
brought home.

                    EILEEN
I wouldn't care if he brought home a tank. That guy is no
good.

                    TERRY
Everybody respects Peter, he knows all the big shots. Jim
Lavaliere comes in the Jack of Diamonds all the time and
hangs out with Peter.

                    EILEEN
Who's Jim Lavaliere?

                    TERRY
He only used to be the Captain of the Celtics, that's all.

                    EILEEN
Peter's a bartender, how could he get you a job?

> *(JOE enters the living room
> wearing fishing gear and
> carrying a bucket. He is a man
> of medium height who was
> strikingly handsome when he
> was younger. He still dresses
> in a style reminiscent of his
> own adolescence in the '50's:
> tightish pants, white socks,
> greaser haircut.)*

TERRY
Everybody drinks in that bar.

EILEEN
Sure, your father's been drinking there for twenty years. I don't want you bothering him with any of this.

TERRY
You're scared he's going to say I can quit and take the job.

EILEEN
Tee, you're not quitting, and I don't want him feeling that the whole family's falling apart just because he's out of work for a while.

TERRY
For a year, you mean.

> *(EILEEN can't speak because JOE enters the kitchen, but she glares at TERRY.)*

JOE
(In good humor, carrying a pail.) Hello everybody. Don't all smile at once.

EILEEN
(Forcing a smile.) Looks like you been fishing.

TERRY
Smells like it too.

JOE
(With humor.) Nice thing to say to your father. Be glad I wasn't out catching skunks.

EILEEN
Any luck?

JOE

(Pulls fish out of the bucket.) Four pound flounder, biggest catch on the whole beach ... What's the matter with the two of you? I'd say the cat got your tongue but we don't have a cat ... And that's good because then the cat would get the fish. Never knew a cat filled up by just a little tongue.

EILEEN

It's just I'm tired, Joe. It is a beautiful catch.

JOE

You know I remember when fish was cheap. It's what we'd have every Friday and in between when we were broke. Now it costs as much as meat. It's like pulling up a five dollar bill on your line.

EILEEN

(Anticipating the work.) You didn't clean it.

JOE

(Annoyed.) Nope, didn't clean it yet. What's going on here? It's like a funeral. I know, you're both in mourning for the fish.

TERRY

(Responding to a look from EILEEN, humors his father with a question.) Where'd you go? Over to Castle Island?

JOE

(Delighted with the question.) Yeah, right out there where it starts to curve into the Bay. Got there just before the tide started coming in. I figured I'd use real heavy sinkers, you know, cast out real far ...

> *(JOE senses neither is listening. TERRY and EILEEN sit hunched. Occasionally each eyes the other. After a silence.)*

What's with the two of you? Okay, what did I do wrong?

EILEEN

(Overly agreeable.) No, it's wonderful you got a fish. I'm just real tired ...

JOE

From **work**. Sure. What is it, Eileen, the job? No, I didn't get a job today.

(Begins to pace.)

EILEEN

Joe, I didn't mean that.

JOE

What am I, some kind of fool? A man comes in and his family practically ignores him --

TERRY

(Interrupts, angry.) It's got nothing to do with you.

(Catches himself, calmer.)

When you came in we were talking about --

EILEEN

Terry!

JOE

(Looks at each.) Yeah, you were talking about?

TERRY

I'm sick of school, I hate it. I want to quit and get a job.

JOE

(As if attacked.) What did you tell him, Eileen? Your lazy father won't work, so you go out and get a job. That's why Cathy never calls. You all think I'm some kind of bum.

TERRY

*(TERRY looks to EILEEN to stop JOE; she just stares back at
TERRY as if she had known all along what JOE's reaction
would be. Then trying to talk sense.)* Dad, what else am I
going to do? I hate school.

EILEEN

You **need** a high school diploma to get a job.

JOE

(Getting angry.) What makes you think you can walk right
out and grab a job when I been trying for a year?

(Proudly.)

Listen, I got a class one license. In twenty years driving
experience, I never had one accident.

TERRY

Peter Thibault is gonna get me a job with the city.

JOE

That's bullshit ... Sure, Peter works for Sculley. He can fix
your parking ticket. If we had a damn car. A job with the
city? Don't make me fall down laughing. Listen, do you know
what number I am on the MTA list? Number 2009. That
means there's two thousand and eight guys ahead of me for a
job with the Transit Authority. Sure you'll get a job with the
city. Why don't you run for Mayor? If I was working, we
wouldn't hear any talk about you leaving school.

TERRY

You're not listening to what I'm telling you.

JOE

Say it! Come right out and say it, goddamn it, both of you.
My lazy father don't work. He fishes all day.

(To EILEEN.)

Say it. My husband can't find a job so he stands out in the water up to his knees. We're gonna lose the house for the taxes, so we have to send our son out to work.

EILEEN
Joe, please! I know you'll get a job.

JOE
A job? We both know what job you're talking about. I know what you want me to do. Crawl to the Casey's on my belly.

TERRY
Dad, this has nothing to do with you. Michael and me –

JOE
I'll go out with my scrub bucket every night like my great grandmother fresh off the boat. Least I'd be out of the house. Least I'd be bringing home money instead of fish, right?

TERRY
(Trying to be heard.) Why shouldn't I get a chance to make money? I got a right to have clothes. I got to bum cigarettes all the time. You want me to go out stealing? Then you'd really be mad.

JOE
(Oblivious.) I am not a nigger and I'm not taking a nigger job so both of you and our goddamn stuck-up daughter in Virginia can go to hell!

> *(Sits. Puts his head in his hands as if to shut them out.)*

EILEEN
(Gets to her feet slowly.) I never said a word about that job of Keith's. I haven't said one word all week.

TERRY

Nobody listens to me in this house, ever! Damn it, this is what you always do. Everytime something goes wrong, you make it out like we're blaming you.

GINA

(At the kitchen door.) Hello, Eileen?

> *(They pay no attention.)*

JOE

Just like your mother. Always ganging up on me. She'll do anything to protect you. You could shoot Father Boyle and she'd find some excuse. But nothing I do is good enough!

TERRY

Aw ...

> *(Starts to say FUCK YOU; glances at EILEEN. Thinks better of it and storms out, almost running into GINA at the door.)*

GINA

(Stands in the doorway now. She wears a white dental assistant's uniform with a red coat slung over her shoulders and a bright scarf holding back her long hair.) Hey, Eileen! Hi, Terry.

> *(TERRY brushes past her as she speaks. Leaves.)*

What?

EILEEN

(Goes to the door.) Oh. Hi, Gina. Listen, this isn't a good time.

GINA

Is something wrong?

EILEEN

Nothing, it's just not a good time to talk.

GINA

I just wanted to know if you'll come to that meeting tonight at Shanahan's, over one street.

EILEEN

(Distracted.) What meeting?

> *(Looks back at JOE.)*

GINA

Eileen, I talked to you about it yesterday. A bunch of parents in the neighborhood. We want to have some voice in the schools, what with Iris having this big rally Sunday with her troublemakers.

EILEEN

I can't go. Look, I can't talk now. I'm sorry.

> *(Starts to walk away. Turns back.)*

Gina, can you cut my hair? Before Saturday, that's my birthday.

> *(She pats at it distractedly.)*

It's all straggly. Some evening?

GINA

(Stares at JOE, fuming at the table.) Sure, tomorrow night. I'll come over after I get the kids to bed.

> *(Leaves.)*

EILEEN

Where's Tee gone? What's happening to him?

> *(She hovers, between the door and JOE. Then slowly goes to*

> *stand behind JOE. She tries*
> *to get through to him as he*
> *sits rigid and cold, resisting*
> *her.)*

I know what you're thinking, Joe, but you're wrong. I **know** you'll find work. If I ever suggested you take Keith up on that job, it's only for a little while. Just to tide us over.

JOE

They're gonna shut the phone off. Don't you be calling Cathy. Let her call us. Her husband makes more in a week than I used to bring home in a month.

EILEEN

(Standing behind him, she begins kneading his shoulders and neck. It is part massage and part caress. Her voice is a lullaby.) You were the best worker the company ever had. Everybody knows that. I remember the first time I saw you driving the warehouse truck. You could take that truck anywhere ...

> *(JOE begins to loosen. Leans*
> *back against her hands.)*

Remember the time you drove the rig down the street here and U-turned it in the driveway, and all the neighbors were hanging out the windows watching? ... Mr. McKay told me nobody could drive a rig like you can. You can't help it when they close down a whole warehouse and move it away. You were the best driver they had ...

> *(As the lights dim, EILEEN*
> *comforts him partly by words*
> *and partly by touch. She*
> *looks weary and spent. Our*
> *last image of EILEEN is of a*
> *woman completely drained --*
> *as if a transfer of her energy*

*has occurred before our eyes
and it is now **he** who is
moving and she who is wan
and transfixed. He turns and
wordlessly clutches her.)*

◆ ◆ ◆

scene 5

*About 7:30 PM on the bar
side of Sculley's Jack of
Diamonds Bar and Steak
House. The room is old but
not run down. It is a
respectable neighborhood
men's tavern. There is a long
bar at which men stand, a
table or two, a dart board to
the side of the bar. Behind
the bar is a telephone. To the
side is a sign that reads
Entrance to Steak House.*

*It is before regulars arrive.
JOE is nursing a beer. PETER
is behind the bar, preparing
for the night's business. He
is wearing a fitted print shirt,
open at the collar enough to
expose the top of his chest. As
the lights come up, JOE is telling
PETER a story.*

JOE

... and then I says to myself, that car belongs to none other than my S.O.B. uncle, Matthew T. Casey and they're fixing to tow it. It's Thursday and Matt's getting his regular haircut and shave at Tommy's across the street. Everybody knows he falls asleep in that chair as soon as he sits down.

> *(JOE enjoys his story and gestures throughout.)*

So they're prying open the little side window. I says to myself, well, maybe I'll take a little stroll across the street and tell old Matt about his car. Mother of God, I thought I'd die laughing. Just as they're hoisting up the front end I see this screaming banshee running across the street. It's old Matt wearing a towel around his neck and the sheet blowing in the wind and his face all covered with shaving cream. Old Tommy the barber's chasing him, waving his razor.

PETER

(Mildly amused.) They tow it?

JOE

Nah, they didn't tow it. Soon as the old geezer wiped the cream off his face and they saw who it was, they just let the car down as if they were inspecting it for him. They wouldn't rip up the ticket, though. Serves him right.

PETER

(Amused.) If Keith hears you say that, your ass is grass.

JOE

(Nearly a mumble.) Yeah, like father, like son ... I hear **you** been doing okay.

PETER

Got no complaints.

JOE

No complaints, huh? Aren't we modest today, Peter Thibault.
You can't be the biggest stud around without people talking,
can you?

PETER

(Swells. Occupies more space along the bar.) I do all right.

JOE

Oh, you do better than all right! Look at those muscles ...
You got a nice car, your own apartment ... I even hear you got
connections now. You been doing favors for people.

PETER

*(This last remark makes PETER curious and somewhat
annoyed.)* What are you talking about?

> *(Phone rings. He stares at JOE,
> then answers it.)*

Slow night, yeah ... Well, it's not even 7:30. You'll be here at
nine? ... Yeah, if he comes in I'll have him wait for you.

> *(JOE picks the darts out of the
> board on the wall and starts to
> play.)*

I'm gonna tell him what we talked about. Maybe we can do
business with the Bitch, but he's got to kick in a little ... No,
nobody's here, don't worry.

> *(Hangs up. Turns to JOE.)*

Now what are you talking about? Favors, connections ...

JOE

Look, Peter, it's no secret to anybody I been out of work for
over a year. Now I'm a good driver. Nobody can drive a rig
like me. I'm reliable ...

PETER

What's that got to do with me?

*(KEITH enters, stands at the
far end of the bar. KEITH is
a young man imitating an
older man. He grew up in the
neighborhood but believes
because of his education and
the years he spent away he can
use his position as accountant
in the family business to move
into being a developer. He
wears a three-piece suit and
carries an attache case.)*

JOE
(Glances at KEITH. Quiet and humble.) I hear you been
helping guys get jobs with the city.

PETER
(Loud.) What do you think I am, the Department of Public
Works? I'm a bartender, that's all.

JOE
(Embarrassed.) Forget it, okay? Forget I ever asked.

PETER
(To KEITH.) Hey, your cousin's seeing double. I'd say he had
too much to drink but he's still on his first beer.

JOE
Shut up about it by now.

PETER
He thinks I look like the Mayor. He asked me to get him a job
with the city.

KEITH
(Walks over to JOE.) What's the matter with the job my
father offered you? Too good to work for the family?

JOE

What kind of job is that for a guy like me? I got twenty years experience, come on.

(Attacks.)

Hey, the old man die? You look like you been to a funeral.

KEITH

He'll see you under, Joe, He's more alive than you are, moping around.

JOE

So how come you look like you're running for Congress?

KEITH

Then I should've worn a better suit, 'cause I'm running for President. If the Kennedys can do it, why can't we? Want to be my campaign manager?

PETER

Now there's a job for you, Joe.

KEITH

(Seriously.) We don't care if you take the job or not, Joe. You're family and the Caseys take care of their own. But there's only one position open at the store and that's custodial.

JOE

A janitor. A goddamn janitor.

PETER

(To KEITH.) Could you hold the family reunion later? My boss wants to buy you a drink.

KEITH

(Turns away.)

Where is Sculley, under the bar? A double shot of Johnny Walker Black.

*(PETER pours his drink at the
end, motions for KEITH to
join him.)*

(Goes to the other end of the bar.) Look, Peter, no use you
trying to hit me again for Iris's campaign. I talked it over with
my father and my uncle. We're in the hardware business.
We're not financing the old battleaxe's comeback single-
handed.

PETER
(Taps KEITH's lapel.) So how'd the bank like your suit?
They advance you any money on it?

KEITH
Money's tight now, they're being cautious, but this block is a
prime location. I could see they were impressed by the
architect's plans.

PETER
They're not going to advance you a cent. Sculley says the
bank's got the neighborhood figured to tip. Come ten years
you're going to be the only white face for miles. This'll be a
whole block of empty renovated stores ..... beautiful,
beautiful.

KEITH
We've been running a business in this neighborhood for
thirty-seven years. Everybody on this block – including
Sculley – is coining money. You think the bank is going to
hold out on us on account of four colored families?

PETER
Three ... There used to be four. With a little persuasion we
got it down to three.

KEITH
We run a legitimate business. We're not getting mixed up with
your street gangs.

PETER

Money's like electricity, it runs things but you don't ask where it comes from. Iris's interests are the same as yours: to keep this neighborhood white.

KEITH

If my wife heard me talking about this, I wouldn't get laid for a year.

PETER

If you don't eat at home, you eat in a restaurant.

KEITH

None of that for me, you never know who's been in the kitchen.

PETER

What the hell do you let Gina bring your kids over to those spades' house for? Don't you know everybody in the neighborhood is watching?

KEITH

She had that kid Suzanne babysitting for her on Saturdays, but my mother nearly had a heart attack and told her to stop.

PETER

That's not what I hear from the neighbors. It's not too cool, man, it's not going to be safe around there. But I guess your wife does what she wants to, huh, Keith?

KEITH

You mind the bar. My wife is my own business.

PETER

Not if she keeps up with this Parent-Council shit.

(Quoting a slogan, maliciously.)

'Black and white unite, to fight for better schools.' She's beginning to make trouble, and people don't like it.

(JOE gets up to leave.)

(To JOE.) No time for your second drink? *(To KEITH.)* I never seen a guy like him. Two-Beer Burke we call him. Hey, Joe, don't it get stale sitting in the glass for two hours?

JOE
(Comes over slowly.) Nah, it needs a little aging. The horse just pissed it out an hour ago. Okay, give me a second draught. Unless you're buying Johnny Walker Black for everybody.

> *(Lights are dimming during the last speech and coming up on scene vi.)*

◆ ◆ ◆

scene 6

Thursday night about 8 PM. EILEEN sits in a chair in the BURKE kitchen with a towel pinned around her as GINA cuts her hair. GINA wears jeans and a peasant blouse; EILEEN, a house dress.

EILEEN
Terry's convinced all he has to do is quit and he'll get a job and a car and his pockets bulging with money and Joe's sure I set him to it. Men are a stubborn lot.

GINA

It's not just the Casey men are hard, if you haven't noticed.
Keith's mother never lets me alone. Eight years we been
married, who else remembers two months?

EILEEN

If it wasn't jumping the gun a bit, it'd be something else.
Mary never laid eyes on a woman she thought was good
enough for Keith. And you being Italian, that sends her up.
Keith was the first of the Casey boys to marry out of the
neighborhood.

GINA

That woman is on my case. She keeps telling me I don't
know how to raise my kids. Her idea is you spoil them with
candy and scare them with stories about hell.

EILEEN

Are you real sorry you moved here?

GINA

It's no good living in his mother's house. When Liquitronics
folded and we couldn't keep up the mortgage, Keith was
down. Two drinks before dinner, asleep on the couch by
nine with the TV on. Now he eats and sleeps the family
business. For years it was, 'The family's so narrow.' Now his
father's next to the Pope, every word he speaks is good
enough to read in Church.

EILEEN

You look so sad when you talk about him? You been
fighting a lot?

GINA

Some.

(Hands her the mirror.)

Want it shorter?

EILEEN

Then it won't need doing again so soon ... Sometimes you go through a rough stretch when all you do is fight.

GINA

Nothing is good enough about me any more. Not the way I dress, not the way I wear my hair. He even gets mad about me going to meetings at the school. But when I skip a meeting, he's at the bar or over at his uncle's or downstairs with his mother ... I worry about that school. Vic can't read a word more than he could last year.

EILEEN

Gina, what do you know about this bussing? Is Terry going to be bussed to Roxbury next year?

GINA

They probably won't say for sure till the last minute. I don't think so, but they sure won't let us know ahead.

EILEEN

I never knew any Blacks before I went to work. We're close in the pool, we cover for each other. Audrey and Lucille got kids, they got money problems, they got troubles with their husband no different than me. I haven't had a woman to talk to every day since Cathy got married and moved to Virginia ...

GINA

Do you ever see Audrey after work? You could invite her over.

EILEEN

You got to be kidding. In this neighborhood? Joe would never stand for it.

GINA

Half these people, they never talked to a Black person in their lives ... Do you know Rosetta Douglas down the block?

EILEEN
We say hello.

GINA
If I didn't have you and Rosetta, I'd sure be lonely. I hardly see Keith now they're cooking up that scheme to renovate their block. I just wish we could move into one of those apartments I saw in the plans.

EILEEN
Gina, this has nothing to do with you, but Joe got cheated out of a share in the hardware store. They never gave Joe's mother anything. Casey and **Sons**.

GINA
That's what Keith is, all right, a son of a Casey.

> *(Snips with a scissors in the air.)*

You know what ticks me off? One night I went down to the bar. I thought, why not? We used to go out together. I walked in and all those guys stared at me like I'd jumped out of a cake. Keith was mortified.

EILEEN
Joe's there every night. Not 'cause he's a drinking man, he isn't. He'll hang out in that bar from seven till midnight and come home sober as he left. Now he's not working, I never see him at night.

GINA
Why not come to the Parents Council, instead of stewing home alone? We're trying to set up block groups, so that if there's more bussing in the fall, people can talk about the facts instead of going crazy on rumors.

EILEEN

(Shrugs it off.) That's not for me ... It wasn't so bad when
Tee was younger. We were close, not like other mothers and
sons. Now he's out every night and I never know what he's
doing. He can't leave school and be a bum.

GINA

The schools are lousy. I'm sure Terry feels cheated anyhow --

EILEEN

He needs a jacket, he needs a shirt, he needs shoes. I can't
give him pocket money. You used to be able to get a job
after school.

GINA

He feels like he doesn't have what he wants to begin with.
Then some troublemaker comes and tells him the Blacks are
going to take that little away.

EILEEN

I got to get this straight about bussing. Saturday morning
I'll go to Little City Hall.

GINA

Do what you want, but all you're gonna get from them is
eight reasons to vote for Iris Mayo Teague.

> *(Hands her the mirror again.)*

You have such pretty hair.

EILEEN

Yeah, it's about all I got left. Let me pay you.

> *(Goes to her purse.)*

Joe used to be wild about my hair. Said it looked like
strawberries and honey. Jesus, that man could talk.

> *(Fumbles with her broken
> purse.)*

I'm gonna lose what little money I got through this hole.

GINA

(Lights dim as GINA talks and come up on other side of the stage.) Maybe it just gets harder, in marriage. Is that how it is? At first he's crazy in love with you and so he tries, but after a while, it's just you trying?

> *(Lights are dimming during the last speech and coming up on scene vii.)*

scene 7

MICHAEL THIBAULT's room, Thursday, 9:00 PM. The stage is dark. A distorted but recognizable voice is heard in a one-sided conversation. Another voice giggles. Gradually lights come up during the first speech on a comfortable place: well lit, nicely furnished and crowded with clothes left all over, pictures, telephone, TV set, radio, stereo.

MICHAEL

(A white exaggeration of Black speech.) Hello, Gina baby ... This is the Big Black Bopper ... I want you to run on over here and suck on my dick. I hears you likes to suck black cock ... She hung up.

TERRY

(Titillated.) What'd she say? I can't believe you did that. Man, you're crazy ... Hey, call Nordella.

MICHAEL

You do it. What are you scared of?

TERRY

Give me the phone.

(He dials.)

Hello, Pizza Shack? ... I want to order five pizzas to be delivered to 10 Holland Street, Dorchester ... What do I want on them?

MICHAEL

Dogshit and cow piss.

TERRY

(Covering the phone.) Shut up ... Uh, raw onion, lots of hot peppers.

MICHAEL

Anchovies.

TERRY

Anchovies. The name? Nordella, Robert Nordella. Could you send them in a hurry, we're having a party here?

(Slams the phone down with laughter.)

MICHAEL

See how easy it was? Just think of that sucker opening his front door. Ready to call the niggers?

TERRY

What are you gonna say?

MICHAEL

Who says it's gonna be me?

TERRY

I aint doing that, I don't know what to say.

MICHAEL

(Slowly as if twisting a knife.) Well, I don't know what to say to Peter when I ask him about getting you a job.

TERRY

This aint no job. What am I gonna tell my parents, that I got a job making phoney calls at night?

MICHAEL

Listen, Peter can get you a great job reading water meters. I talked to him about it this morning. There's not a kid in the city wouldn't do **anything** for that job.

TERRY

So what do I got to make some stupid phone call for?

MICHAEL

You get the job after we've done our job. It's up to us to clean this place out. WHIP is looking for guys who aren't afraid to fight for what they think.

TERRY

What's WHIP?

MICHAEL

Peter thought it up. W.H.I.P. White Homeowners in Patriotism. It's the organization, man, our organization. And you and me, we're in it from the start.

> *(He sees a vision.)*

We're gonna walk down the streets in our insignia and everybody's gonna know who we are. You know how when a cop walks into Sculley's steak house, they fall all over him. Sculley sends him over a Porterhouse steak for free. It'll be like that for us. Our job is to do what the cops won't do.

> *(He takes a five-dollar bill from his pocket. Hands it to TERRY.)*

Get me two cans of black and two cans of red spray paint.
Meet me in front of Sculley's at eleven.

TERRY
What for?

MICHAEL
Just be there at eleven with the paint. And I want receipts ...
Now listen good. I'm gonna do one more to show you how.
Let's say you want to scare some chick. I hope that bitch
Suzanne answers.

(He dials.)

TERRY
What are you gonna say?

MICHAEL
Shit, it's busy ... I'm gonna tell her the next time you're home
alone, don't bother to lock the door because we'll come in
through the window, and when we get done with you, you're
gonna piss blood for a week.

TERRY
Hey, let's call Darlene.

MICHAEL
You do it.

TERRY
(Dials the phone. Disguises his voice.) Hello, Mrs. Ross? Can
I speak to Darlene ... This is Mr. Nordella.

MICHAEL
Yeah, tell her to come on over and eat pizza.

TERRY
Oh. No thanks.

(Hangs up.)

She's out. Probably with that faggot from B.C. I'd like to smash him right in the face.

MICHAEL
Why, because she won't go out with you any more?

TERRY
She won't go out with anybody who's not rich and don't have a car.

MICHAEL
That leaves you out. Maybe I'll call her up.

TERRY
Sure, you could call her up and say, this is Baby Huey, you want to go out with me? That's what she used to call you ... Call the niggers again.

MICHAEL
(Dials and hangs up.) Still busy.

> *(A silence. MICHAEL's silence is one of contentment. He is the 'Lord of the Manor' in his room and he gazes about it proudly. His weapon, the telephone, is on his lap. TERRY is visibly worried.)*

TERRY
My mother's birthday is this week.

MICHAEL
Make her a present in woodworking.

TERRY
Shut up. I want to get her something good ... You think you could let me have ten dollars?

MICHAEL
You want me to rip off a present for her like I did the radio?

TERRY
You didn't rip that off. We both did ... Come on, I'll pay you back. I don't want to steal my mother's birthday present.

MICHAEL
I'll give you eight bucks, but I want it back.

(Lights dim.)

scene 8

Lights come up. We see the DOUGLAS family living room with a partial view of the kitchen. ROSETTA is making a dress. It is put together but not hemmed. SUZANNE sits sideways on the easy chair polishing her fingernails and toenails. Her books are on the floor beside her, open. Both are hungry, mindful of FRANKLIN's cooking.

SUZANNE
(Raising her voice.) Franklin, was that duck dead before you started? We've been waiting an hour and a half.

ROSETTA
(Evident from her posture that she is very tired. She has her shoes off and is a little cranky.) Come on, let the boy try.

Don't care if I eat or not, I'm so beat ... Whose nail polish is that?

FRANKLIN
(He is in the kitchen cooking an elaborate supper. As he passes back and forth near the doorway, he can hear the conversation between ROSETTA and SUZANNE at times, and he sometimes responds.) Fifteen more minutes! This is worth waiting for!

SUZANNE
Yours. Called Forest Fire. Mama, you know I'm not gonna use up my babysitting money for nail polish.
(Conspiratorial.)
You call him in here. I'll run and steal the peanut butter and crackers. This could go on all night. If he went to engineering school, I wouldn't care if he took a year to build a bridge, but I'm starving.

ROSETTA
Try on this dress. I want to start pinning the hem. Franklin too tired last night, he forgot to defrost the duck. Let him show off, honey. I don't mind your using my things, but you got to ask.

SUZANNE
(Not wanting to try on the dress.) Consider yourself asked ... Okay, I'll write my stupid report on hunger in Appalachia. I'm in the mood.

ROSETTA
How come you won't try the dress? Otherwise it'll never be ready on time for awards night. I couldn't bear for you to go up on the stage in front of all those people in your old dress, and it's too short on you anyhow.

SUZANNE

I can wear a skirt and blouse. Don't go overboard. It's not like they're giving me anything. Just a piece of pasteboard with a sticker.

ROSETTA

Gonna be a beautiful dress. Just like you showed me in the magazine. I got to stick at it and not lose my temper cutting and piecing, but I can copy anything ...

(She is coming back to life.)

You get your artistic side from me. Your Daddy was a strong man. If he needed to, he could move a house. But he didn't have no delicate artistic hand. More like a sledgehammer ...

(Glances out the window. Stares. Then turns back, relaxed again.)

Just the people next door.....Sometimes I think he was a fool, too, Franklin, Sr. Such a proud man. You know what he used to say? In twenty years it won't be no different being Black to being Eyetalian or Irish or Portugee.

FRANKLIN

He sure was wrong about living here. It's lonely as ever. Now the Johnson's split, I never see Alida no more.

SUZANNE

Why don't you ask her out? You got to have her served up on a platter like that Duck Bigelow?

FRANKLIN

(Pronouncing it correctly.) Bigaraude! Bigaraude!

SUZANNE

I don't care how wide the street is. Call her up. She got a phone like everybody else.

FRANKLIN

You know you are ignorant. You get a tuna fish sandwich tonight. Mama and me will split the duck.

ROSETTA

Why not call her? You never were bashful before.

FRANKLIN

She gonna go out with me Saturday night and watch me bus tables at the Oyster House? I work Friday and Saturday and Sunday. She's gonna think I'm crazy if I ask her for a date on Monday night.

SUZANNE

I wouldn't care if some brother called me up for Monday morning to watch the Today show. Even Mama's got a boyfriend. Hey, when you gonna go out with that Curtis again? I saw you kiss and make up on the front porch.

ROSETTA

I hope the neighbors didn't watch with you. Suzanne, don't fuss over it. Did you like me bringing him home to supper? It's of no account. Just I thought why not, he some kind of company and he fixed the window.

> *(She glances out the window again, over her shoulder. Looks for a moment, holding that position. Then,satisfied, turns back.)*

SUZANNE

Sure, no account. You bring home men for supper every forty years or so, it's a regular thing like Haley's Comet.

ROSETTA

Well, how many men do I meet? Not a lot of good unmarried Black men come trucking into a dry goods store buying

flowered polyester by the yard. Besides, I don't know what
I'm doing with a man six years younger than me anyhow.

SUZANNE

After thirty, what difference does it make?

ROSETTA

Remember when you thought sixteen was grown up? ... Don't
know that I feel real grown up yet. Times when I was out on
the street with you and Franklin by the hand, I used to feel
like I was playing mother. Guess I think of grown-ups as
them, they settled, they gave up.

SUZANNE

Wish we could give up and just live ... We got to fight every
day.

> *(Louder, so FRANKLIN can
> hear.)*

But like they say, an army fights on its stomach and this
army is starving.

> *(Once again, ROSETTA
> glances out the window, then
> turns back.)*

FRANKLIN

Five minutes. Did you set the table yet, did you even set the
table? Tuna fish for you.

> *(Phone rings. ROSETTA goes
> to answer. She talks inaudibly
> until spot comes up on
> CURTIS.)*

SUZANNE

> *(Goes into kitchen with
> FRANKLIN. Starts to carry*

> *dishes from kitchen to living*
> *room.)*

For a hot duck, it sure stayed cold a long time.

FRANKLIN

Shut your mouth. She'll hear you.

SUZANNE

What did you tell her, you found it on the bus?

FRANKLIN

You shush. Told her they had an extra one left over at work.
I want her to have something nice for once.

> *(Spot comes up on CURTIS*
> *against a bar backdrop. He is*
> *calling from an open payphone,*
> *music behind him.)*

CURTIS

Guess what fell on me? I won the Easter turkey at work. How
about you come over to my house and do something
wonderful to my bird.

ROSETTA

All you got to do is pop it in the oven for a while.

CURTIS

I don't know nothing about turkeys except that I work with
them all day. Come on, I'll get a bottle of wine for Friday
night. We both need a good time after we put in a hard week.
Then you can take half the turkey home for your kids. How
about that?

ROSETTA

For the sake of the children, how can I say no?

CURTIS

You gonna be busy later on? I might just drop over.

ROSETTA

Franklin's cooking up a fancy French duck he studied in school. I never ate a duck in my life. Want us to save you some?

CURTIS

Look, baby, I'll give you a call later on if I can get away. But I'll pick you up Friday after work.

(ROSETTA hangs up.)

SUZANNE

(As she sets the table.) Curtis coming over?

ROSETTA

If he can get away.

SUZANNE

From what?

ROSETTA

Now how do I know from what? Work, I guess.

SUZANNE

At night?

ROSETTA

Suzanne, one thing about men you just getting to know, you don't go asking too many questions. Just like them not to tell you nothing till the last minute, like you the bottom line on their list they got to do, and they won't do it if something better comes up.

SUZANNE

Was Daddy like that?

ROSETTA

At first. Something holds them back. Like the minute they say they love you, they think they gonna be stuck for life in

some tub of molasses, just drowning and watching the sweet
world go by.

SUZANNE

Some men changing, Mama. Not everybody is into playing
those old games.

ROSETTA

I heard that one before, how the world changing. Your Daddy
sure of that. He'd walk down this block proud as a tuba
player. He'd say, 'Hi, neighbor, glad to meet you,' but you
know they were not glad to meet him.

SUZANNE

I don't know how many of them I'm ever glad to meet.

> *(Takes a seat at the dining
> table.)*

ROSETTA

(She is fully animated by now. Acts out this story.) I wish I
had a movie camera today. I call it, Here Come Your Black
Neighbor, Smile You on Candid Camera. Maureen out there
on her front lawn with her crabby husband. He tell her, put
it there, Maureen, no, not there, here. She see me coming and
she start to say hello. Then she look at him and she think
better of it. She pretend she looking at a bird up in the tree.

> *(Imitates.)*

She looking straight up, acting like she so interested she don't
happen to see me. Then just as I come up to her, she look
down. Whoops, there I am, big as life. She sort of twitch, she
look at her husband. Finally she flash some stupid smile – not
at me but right at the tree. So I give the tree a big smile and
sail on by.

FRANKLIN

Today when I was passing Joey's, couple of ignoramus white

boys followed me down the block yelling, Hey big nigger, after me.

> *(Marching deliberately back and forth in the kitchen as he cooks.)*

Mama, don't give up, Old Donald Duck has quacked his last.

ROSETTA
Don't you fight them, Franklin. It don't solve a thing, just make it worse.

SUZANNE
Mama, it's getting worse all by itself. They're fighting us, why shouldn't we fight them?

FRANKLIN
Always got to be proving something over and over ... They always pick me out, all through school, look at that **big** Black boy, he ought to play football. Look at that **big** Black there, he ought to box.

SUZANNE
You know why I like Curtis? He's a scrapper, like Daddy.

ROSETTA
Mmmm. Your Daddy fight like the Lord on his side, he gotta win. Curtis a guerrilla fighter. He figure he gonna be operating against the odds for a long, long time.

FRANKLIN
I want to fight like an elephant, that just walk on through the opposition and keep moving ... I want a job where I feel good, where I please people, make them mellow.

SUZANNE
Great, invite those punks in for duck. Stuff it with rocks.

FRANKLIN

They hopeless. Down the block they have fun by sitting
around staring at the TV and throwing beer cans at each other.

ROSETTA

Turning into a snob. Used to be I never know how you tasted
it, the food go straight from the fork to your belly.

FRANKLIN

They all brain damaged anyhow. You always fed us good, no
matter what. Not the fancy cooking I'm laying out but good
victuals. But those honkies, they eat Sugar Pops and Ring
Dings and Fritos. They probably all got protein deficiency in
the brain. I was studying about that at school, and I figure
it fits them to a T around here. That's why they so mean and
weird.

SUZANNE

I got protein deficiency and low blood sugar and spots in front
of my eyes and beri beri and scurvy and all that sickness comes
from starvation in the advanced stages ... Course if I don't get
word on that scholarship soon, I'm gonna kill myself anyhow.

ROSETTA

(Puts down the dress.) Don't joke like that. Don't never say
that, even for a joke.

> *(Shakes her head at SUZANNE.
> She is mad.)*

My mama spent fifty years cleaning house for stuck-up
crackers, getting up at six and taking the MTA two trains and
then a bus all the way to Arlington to clean their pig sty. So
we be housed and fed and clothes on our backs, and so I could
go all the way through high school 'cause she never got to go
through the eighth grade. Every goddamn one of us graduate
high school ...

> *(Walks over to hand the dress to SUZANNE.)*

You gonna get that scholarship 'cause you so smart they can't keep you back. Just like you gonna cross that stage in front of all those people and grab that award, and they can suck lemons. I'm gonna burst with pride. Now you try this on so I can pin the hem.

SUZANNE

(About to give in. Takes the dress and holds it up.) Mama, it's beautiful! But it just makes me feel bad. Where am I ever gonna go in this dress?

FRANKLIN

(Stands in the doorway.) Hold on! Everybody was on my back, and now dinner's ready and you want to stage a fashion show.

SUZANNE

After this feast, I'll be too fat for the dress. You want me to carry something, Franklin?

FRANKLIN

Sit down. Both of you, sit. I'm serving.

> *(Carries each dish to the table separately with dramatic flourishes, showman like.)*

I want to get out of this crazy place. Somewhere people live decent.

> *(Carries in another dish.)*

One of them emerging African nations. Now you figure they got to bring in tourists. Where you got tourists, you need first class hotels and deluxe restaurants and fancy cooking.

> *(Stands in the doorway with*

the duck. Poses with it on high.)

Here I come strolling in slow and easy wearing all white from head to toe with a chef's hat on looking eight feet tall and smiling, just a little, very dignified, like I know I really rolled them in the aisles, and as I wait, they all burst into applause ...

ROSETTA

(Phone rings. She jumps up.) That'll be Curtis. Just gonna tell him to scoot over and share the feast....Hello, Curtis honey?....Who is this?....What?

(Her voice rises in agitation.)

Who is this?....Who is this?

(Lights dim. End of ACT ONE.)

ACT 2

scene 1

Friday morning about 9:00 AM. GINA and KEITH CASEY in their kitchen, a large recently renovated room in an old triple-decker frame house. Having just returned from taking the kids to school, GINA is hurriedly preparing to go to work. She wears her dental assistant's uniform. KEITH sits at the kitchen table. Spread before him are mortgage applications, account books. He has pushed aside the kids' cereal box, milk container and bowls. The floor is strewn with an asssortment of coloring books, socks and toys.

GINA

Vic's ear is much better this morning.

KEITH

You know that kid. Always complaining about something.
Just like his mother.

GINA

What?

>*(As she continues to clean up.)*

You want scrambled eggs this morning?

KEITH

With salt and pepper and long black hair? No thanks.

GINA

You used to like my hair this way. You said it was sexy.

KEITH

Mother says you look like the last hippie. You have time to
cut everybody else's hair for blocks. You can't still run
around like a college student at thirty.

GINA

Keith, your mother wouldn't like me if I came gold-plated.
Come on, sweetheart, have some breakfast. You'll only go
out and get something at Joey's ... What's wrong?

KEITH

(After silence.) They turned us down yesterday at First City
Bank.

GINA

Is that why you came in so late last night?

KEITH

I had dinner with my father and Uncle Jack. Then I had
business with Sculley.

GINA

Business isn't so bad when you can do it at the bar.

KEITH

I don't like those crooks any better than you do. Peter's the same loudmouth punk he was in high school.

GINA

I'd like to know what makes him such a big man around here.

KEITH

He's a big man in the bar, that's all. Sculley's okay, though. He's a politician from the old school, but at least he knows how to eat his soup without getting it on his shirt.

GINA

How come you need his money? There must be fifty banks in Boston.

KEITH

Mortgage financing is too complicated for me to explain. They want us to account for every damn nail we sell ... I'm tired, Gina.

GINA

But you're always tired. You never have time for me any more.

KEITH

Well, you want to work on the attic this weekend?

GINA

I don't want to put more work into this house. Your mother is going to drive me crazy.

KEITH

(Crosses his arms.) Why didn't you tell me you were bringing the kids to that colored girl on Saturday mornings?

GINA

Why don't you ever ask me what I do with the kids Saturday morning? Why aren't you ever here Saturday morning?

KEITH

Let mother watch them.

GINA

(Gives up trying to make breakfast and sits down, sucked into the argument.) Because all she does is fill them up with cookies all day and let them watch TV till they're bugeyed. At least Suzanne reads to them and takes them outside.

KEITH

How can you pick out the one Black teenager this side of the park? You know how backward people are around here.

GINA

A lot of people don't hate Blacks. So far we have a few people who'll stand up and a lot more who are still scared to. The other side is organized already --

KEITH

What other side?

GINA

We've argued about this time after time. You won't look at what's happening. Just last night I got an obscene phone call ... It turned my stomach.

KEITH

What did he say?

GINA

(Shakes her head.)

KEITH

You stick out like a sore thumb. Stop thinking about yourself for once. Supose Mother had answered the phone?

GINA

(Laughs.) Keith, I don't understand you. You want to stay, I want to move, but you object to every friend I make in the neighborhood, everything I do that helps me feel like I belong.

KEITH

You think it was easy marrying an Italian girl? Why go out of your way to remind them all the time that you're different?

GINA

Keith, I'm not the only different one. At the Parents Council I meet people who think like us. Won't you come with me? People we could invite for dinner.

KEITH

I'm getting to know people who think exactly the opposite. You've hardly considered any other point of view ... You have no right to take the children where there's trouble.

GINA

Trouble? Suzanne takes wonderful care of them. Rosetta's my friend.

KEITH

(Explodes.) I don't want my kids over there! I don't want my wife over there! And I don't want to walk into Sculley's and find out what you've been up to, because every loudmouth in the neighborhood is gossiping about you. I want you to stop right now!

GINA

Why do you have to make a scene just when I leave for work? Damn it, Keith, I can't live this way! You come in after eleven, I'm asleep already, and every morning we get into a fight!

KEITH

Don't change the subject. Are you going to stop?

GINA

(Runs around collecting coat, purse.) Look at you. Look at us. You won't even let me choose the babysitter. You say you're so concerned about the kids, but you won't spend time with them. All you want to do is park them with your mother and ignore what's happening in this neighborhood.

KEITH

I said, are you going to stop?

GINA

(Pauses. Then walks out.) NO!

scene 2

The BURKE household, a little before 11:00 AM Friday. TERRY enters the kitchen carrying a shopping bag labelled CASEY HARDWARE AND HOUSEWARES which he puts down on the table. Hearing JOE snoozing on the couch in the living room, TERRY glances in, then moves quietly about the kitchen so as to avoid JOE. JOE has been in the living room all morning. The newspaper is scattered over the floor. Next to the couch are the telephone, a glass emptied of milk and some plates.

JOE

(Awakens.) Hooking school again. Sure as shit you're gonna end up like me.

TERRY

Can't go back until Monday and I have to have a parent with me. You're gonna have to come unless Mom misses work.

JOE

Sure, unless that job interview with UPS comes through.

>*(Makes himself more presentable,*
>*tucking in his shirt, smoothing*
>*back his hair.)*

Who told you Peter Thibault could get you a job with the city? I hope it wasn't that stupid brother of his. You know I talked to Peter last night.

>*(TERRY enters the living room.)*

He's not gonna do anything for you.

TERRY

He said that?

JOE

He said he didn't have any connections. Not for us anyway.

>*(TERRY leaves the room.)*

Where are you going? I'm only trying to keep you from getting your hopes up, that's all.

TERRY

I got to meet Michael at eleven. I'm gonna be late.

JOE

(Goes into the kitchen after TERRY. JOE tries to put his arm around him.) Are you going to tell me there's not one class in high school you like?

TERRY

(Pulls away.) Dad, I got to meet Michael.

JOE

I called every job in the paper today.

> *(Sits down at the table.)*

Nothing.

TERRY

What about the moving and storage place in Dedham?

JOE

Soon as I told them I had twenty years experience, they said I was too old. I could sue them for that.

> *(Reaches for the package.)*

What's in the bag?

TERRY

(Pulls it away.) Stuff I picked up for Michael.

JOE

You know we get a twenty percent discount at the store on all domestic items ...

TERRY

What do I care, it's Michael's money.

JOE

Want to come fishing with me this afternoon?

> *(JOE gets excited at the prospect. Gets up to look out the window.)*

Looks perfect. Tide starts coming in around twelve-thirty. We could take the bus and be there in --

TERRY

I told you. I got to meet Michael.

JOE

That snivelling kid used to follow you to baseball practice.
Baby Huey, they called him ... Now you think he's such a big
man. You used to beg me to take you fishing. Remember
when some of the guys from the VFW went out fishing on
Memorial Day?

TERRY

I was the only kid on the trip.

JOE

Damn right you were ... It was Walter Ross's big old cabin
cruiser, the Pretty Pauline. Your line wasn't in water five
minutes before you pulled up a flounder. Jesus, those guys
were burning.

TERRY

That was the first time I ever had a beer.

JOE

(Feeling he has finally reached TERRY.) You remember that?
Walter Ross, what a horse's ass. It was his rule, NO WIVES,
NO KIDS. And you know why? Because he didn't want
Pauline or his daughters coming. He was drinking can after
can from the minute we left the dock, and what'd you say?
"Is that tonic for grown-ups?" The second I walked away to
help Tommy the Barber -- he got a hook in his thumb -- Walt
gave you a can of beer and told you to chug it.

TERRY

Everybody was watching. I was scared not to!

JOE

Sure, I came back and you were puking it over the side.

TERRY

(Giggles.) You were so mad you dumped my bucket right
over his head, fish and all.

JOE

Damn right I did. Stupid big shot drunk ... That was the last time Walt ever took me out ... I bet you drink beer now, though, huh?

TERRY

Dad, I got to go.

JOE

Go ahead! Who the hell wants to sit around the house talking to an old man?

TERRY

It's just, I'm late.

JOE

All right, all right.

> *(Takes a dollar out of his pocket.)*

Here, Terry. Take this. Get yourself something.

TERRY

Dad, I don't want anything! You should keep the dollar. You don't like walking around with no money in your pockets.

JOE

(Approaches anger.) Jesus, Mary and Michael, take the damn money. Just let me give you something.

> *(TERRY takes the dollar and leaves.)*

◆ ◆ ◆

scene 3

Outside the Jack of Diamonds. MICHAEL paces as he waits for TERRY. He wears a royal blue coach's jacket. Bolts of lightning are crisscrossed on the back; a round insignia with the letters WHIP emblazons his breast. His walk is an obvious swagger. He seems almost puffed in his new jacket. TERRY, twenty minutes late, enters carrying the hardware store bag.

MICHAEL

Where were you?

TERRY

(Moving closer to read the insignia. Feels the material.)
Where'd you get that?

MICHAEL

You think I got all day to stand around here waiting for you?

TERRY

I was trying to rip it off and save you money, but my uncle was following me around the store. So what, I'm late.

MICHAEL

From now on, if we agree to be somewhere, you be there. What if I was in trouble and needed your help? We're not fooling around any more.

TERRY

Get off my back ... You save one of those jackets for me? Did Peter buy them?

MICHAEL

Maybe you get one and maybe you don't.

*(In full command. Stares
TERRY down.)*

Let me see the stuff.

*(TERRY hands over the
package and while he is
fumbling over the change,
MICHAEL continues.)*

You got the receipts?

TERRY

When can I get a jacket?

MICHAEL

I was just having a beer with my brother. Things are moving
fast. He wants me to get a group of guys together by Sunday
to be marshals at the rally. After that the whole
neighborhood will know what these jackets mean.

TERRY

A marshal? I'll be a marshal. Where's my jacket?

MICHAEL

There's one for every guy I pick. This is just a sample.

(Poses. Turns around.)

Dig the great design on the back. Crossed lightning. That's us,
white lightning when we're crossed.

TERRY

Come on, let me try it on.

MICHAEL

It's too big for you. Maybe they're all too big for you.

TERRY
What are you talking about?

MICHAEL
Think you'll be ready for Sunday?

TERRY
What's going to happen? Is there going to be a fight?

MICHAEL
First we got a little job to do. You'll get a jacket if everything goes all right.

TERRY
What do you want me to do?

MICHAEL
Something you should have done a long time ago. It's right on your block.

◆ ◆ ◆

scene 4

Approximately 8:00 AM on Saturday morning in CURTIS McDONALD's bedroom in an apartment in the Roxbury section of Boston. Early morning light filters through the curtains to illuminate a double bed, a night table and an alarm clock. The alarm sounds. CURTIS is in bed, sleeping. ROSETTA, awake for half an

hour already, crosses buttoning
her dress, to shut it off.

CURTIS

Hey, what in hell?

ROSETTA

Sorry, Curtis. I got something to do this morning.

CURTIS

(Turns over to look at the clock.) Eight AM! Shit, woman, this is the weekend. I sleep late Saturday morning.

ROSETTA

I was thinking we'd have breakfast together. I started the coffee, but if you want to sleep in, honey, go ahead.

CURTIS

Why the hell didn't you think of that before you set the alarm? How am I supposed to sleep with you running all over?

ROSETTA

Now if you can't sleep, why not have some breakfast? I didn't find no bacon, but there's eggs and bread and juice.

CURTIS

Been fixing myself breakfast since I was five. Don't need no woman to make me breakfast.

(Covers his head.)

ROSETTA

Um. Sure different in the morning than last night! Never mind. Got other things to bother my mind than some changeable man.

(Stalks out.)

CURTIS

(Silence. In the next room ROSETTA pours herself coffee and prepares to leave. Then CURTIS uncovers his head.)
Rosetta ... Hey, baby.

ROSETTA

(Calling from the other room.) Go back to sleep. That's all you want, now.

CURTIS

Give me a break, woman. I wake up nasty ... Come here.

> *(ROSETTA comes in wearing her coat and drinking a cup of coffee. She leans on the doorway looking at him, almost pouting.)*

That coffee smells as good as that perfume of yours. Ripple?

ROSETTA

Replique.

> *(She is relenting a little.)*

Want some? I made a pot.

CURTIS

Where'd you get yourself a classy French accent and French perfume? You got another man on the side with a fat wallet?

ROSETTA

Sure, he called Franklin. That's who I was calling last night, every hour on the hour ... I got to go now.

CURTIS

But I want my morning coffee, sweet and black.

ROSETTA

You change your mind fast. Minute ago, you ready to send me down the garbage disposal.

CURTIS

Rosetta, you set my alarm clock without asking me, you wake me at the crack of dawn, you rummage through my kitchen like you been cooking here for years, then you want to make me breakfast. I am not into that domestic routine.

ROSETTA

Now look here, Curtis, I got to go down to the Little City Hall this morning. Make them put pressure on the police before those punks burn my house down. Just because nothing went wrong last night, don't mean my family is in the clear.

(Starts to leave.)

CURTIS

No way you gonna get any help pussyfooting around with the police. Those punks don't scare me. I want to help, but you keep tying my hands behind my back.

ROSETTA

You want to stand up to a whole neighborhood, but you don't even want to eat breakfast with me? Come on, you want a good time, and I don't even know if I can afford you. You like some luxury to me.

CURTIS

Baby, I wasn't born last night. Take a woman home for a little fun and the next thing you know she's making breakfast, moving the furniture around, decorating your whole apartment.

ROSETTA

I got a home of my own, two kids, and a whole boiling pot full of bad troubles. You not my problem, Curtis. You just a little honey on my burnt toast. No way you can help me.

CURTIS

Can't go walking out without even a goodbye kiss. Come here.

> *(ROSETTA saunters over. As she passes the night table, she puts down the empty cup. Sits on the very edge of the bed.)*

Didn't even bring me no coffee. Mean! Selfish and mean!

> *(Grabs her around the waist. Nuzzles her neck.)*

ROSETTA

Listen, three years I ain't gone with a man, so I guess I can wait three more or how long it take to find a man not scared of me.

CURTIS

You never gonna find a man with brains not scared of you. You scarey. But I put up a real good show being brave.

> *(Tickles her.)*

ROSETTA

What you want with me anyhow? Just a middle age woman with grown up kids and a lot of whites trying to drive me crazy.

CURTIS

You know what I want. *(Serious.)* But, baby, I got a life and a place of my own.

ROSETTA

(Laughs. Puts her arms around his neck.) You got endless places of your own. Your mama. Your sister Lorraine, your sister Jo Ellen. Your girlfriend Martha, your girlfriend Samanda --

CURTIS

I can't go to Samanda's no more ... You jealous?

ROSETTA

Of what, honey? A man who act like he camping on a frying pan? Curtis, I ask myself, if you gonna make it harder or you gonna make it easier ...

CURTIS

What kind of woman are you, got me trying to convince you now how good I am to you?

> *(Starts to gently massage her neck, coming on strong.)*

Sweet baby, relax and bring me some coffee and I'll put on a record and we'll have us one Saturday morning.

ROSETTA

(Gently pulls away, holding his head in her hands.) I got to go, honey, I'm sorry.

> *(Strokes his cheek, gets up to leave.)*

CURTIS

(Grabs her arm. The grip is tight, the voice is velvet.) Baby, where are you going now?

ROSETTA

It's after nine. I got to go.

CURTIS

No, baby, you got to stay.

ROSETTA

Curtis, let go my arm. I'm not fooling. I have to go to that damn Little City Hall. You believe I'd rather go there than be with you? Come on over for dinner tonight.

CURTIS

Maybe I got things to do ... All you do is act contrary and I
don't like it. Maybe I'll see you some time next week.

ROSETTA

Curtis, you some revolving door like they got going into the
bank -- you know that? One minute you're coming close, the
next minute you're speeding away. All I know is I got no
time to be going in circles all morning.

(Leaves.)

scene 5

*Saturday morning, a little after
nine in the Little City Hall, a
small store front office serving
as a neighborhood adjunct to
the City Hall downtown.
The furnishings are sparse --
reflecting the taste of its
director as well as its priority as
a city agency -- a desk, some
hard chairs, a flag pole, portraits
of the President Gerald Ford,
President Kennedy and the
Mayor. On one of the chairs is
a large cardboard box filled with
leaflets. The office is empty
except for its Director, frail
MRS. ROSS. She is on the
telephone as the scene opens,*

> *making last minute preparations*
> *for Sunday's neighborhood*
> *rally.*

MRS. ROSS

Yes, that's right, Mr. Guinter. The buses will be there at
11:30. We're having a cook-out in the park and then the
ushers will show you to your block of seats. The buses will
take you back by 4 PM.

> *(Enter PETER. He pantomines*
> *a basketball player to her. She*
> *tries to ignore him as she*
> *continues the phone call.)*

No, Mr. Guinter, yours is not the only home invited. Senior
Citizens from the ...

> *(Checks her list as PETER*
> *continues. She resists but it's*
> *hard to ignore him.)*

Fairview, the Oak Park, Metropolitan Memorial, St. Catherine's,
and the Dorchester Nursing Home are also coming ... You're
entirely welcome. See you at the rally.

> *(Hangs up the phone.)*

Please don't try to interrupt me on the telephone again.

PETER

Tomorrow afternoon at exactly 2:45 PM, a red convertible lent
by Kiley Pontiac and driven by yours truly will pull up to the
speaker's platform. Carrying none other than Jim Lavaliere,
who's gonna deliver a five minute speech on why Iris Mayo
Teague is the only choice for City Councilor. I nailed him.
Worked on that bastard for three weeks.

> *(Sits down on the corner of her*
> *desk, annoying her.)*

MRS. ROSS

(Ostentatiously moves some papers to safety.) I'm sure Mr. Lavaliere would be offended if he heard you refer to him in that manner. I know I am ... He's not the captain of the Celtics **any longer**, is he?

PETER

Iris isn't City Councilor **any longer**, is she?

MRS. ROSS

Peter, there are five hundred more leaflets on the chair. Could you take care of it?

PETER

More?

MRS. ROSS

We're trying to attract two thousand.

PETER

I got twenty kids on the street right now. I was supposed to have thirty. Your daughter was one of the ones who didn't show up.

MRS. ROSS

Were the other nine who didn't show up sixteen-year-old girls? Perhaps their mothers forbid them to pick up leaflets at your apartment.

PETER

What are you talking about? There were twenty kids there.

MRS. ROSS

Your reputation is all over the neighborhood. Darlene's been educated by the Sisters. I don't care for older men pursuing her, and I'm sure John Sculley wouldn't either if I talked to him about it.

> *(PETER stares at her as if she's crazy.)*

Do you know a Mr. Nordella? An Italian?

PETER

Sure, he's a shop teacher at the high school.

MRS. ROSS

Someone called my house last night and gave that name ...

> *(Musing.)*

It sounded a lot like that Burke kid I caught pestering her behind the door at her birthday party ... And let me tell you something, Peter, those hoodlums of yours had better behave themselves this time.

PETER

Don't worry so much. Tomorrow they're all going to be wearing blue jackets and looking real sharp. They won't do nothing without the word from me.

MRS. ROSS

I'm not just talking about the rally, Peter. Your kids are all over this neighborhood causing trouble.

PETER

Take it up with Sculley. If this neighborhood goes, Iris won't get votes if she stands on the corner handing out afro-piks. We're starting a real organization. Did one person in that nigger family get hurt? No. But they sure as hell moved out of here quick. We're getting results, Mrs. Ross.

MRS. ROSS

I'll tell you what you're doing. You're turning out kids to be in gangs such as we haven't seen around here for twenty years. What do you think those kids are going to do once they drive those people out -- you think they're going to forget they were being paid –

PETER
They're not being paid.

MRS. ROSS
Who was it again you wanted that meter reading job for, Peter?

PETER
My brother. Since when do you work for nothing?

MRS. ROSS
Well, he can't have it. Iris had twelve slots this spring, and she's filled them all.

PETER
My brother's been putting up posters and handing out leaflets for two weeks and he's head marshal at the rally. He deserves something.

MRS. ROSS
Perhaps we can get him something with the Parks Department, but it's only for the summer.

>*(EILEEN enters shyly. PETER turns, and seeing her, rises from the desk.)*

PETER
The leaflets are in the box, right?

>*(He does not listen to the conversation but goes to the box, counts the leaflets into piles, stacks them and leaves before ROSETTA enters.)*

MRS. ROSS
Mrs. Burke, this is a surprise. Can we do something for you?

EILEEN

(Sits in the chair beside the desk. Speaks timidly.) You remember my son Terry? He and Darlene used to be friends in the eighth grade. Well, he came home the other night and says he's quitting school ... Because of the bussing.

MRS. ROSS

You're not the only one I've heard that from, dear, believe me. It's happening every day.

EILEEN

He says he's going to have to go to school in Roxbury next fall. Is that true?

MRS. ROSS

We're all in the dark, actually. But I can tell you, Iris Mayo Teague is keeping tabs on what they're trying to pull, and believe me, she's one of the only chances we have. This is strictly off the record, but the Mayor is selling us down the river.

EILEEN

Mrs. Ross, it's true then? Terry's right?

MRS. ROSS

Do you blame him? Do you want your son to change schools in midstream? I know I wouldn't want that for Darlene.

EILEEN

Not changing schools, no. He just has a year to go ... But I work with colored people, and I don't see what all the fuss is.

MRS. ROSS

Mrs. Burke, you grew up in this neighborhood just as I did. Our parents worked hard for what they got. You should know, you married a Casey. We've had a nice neighborhood, we've had a safe neighborhood, we've had our own neighborhood school. We're not against the colored necessarily, we're against anyone who wants to take away what we've worked for and turn this neighborhood into a slum.

EILEEN
It seems like the neighborhood's changing anyhow. The kids are so mad all the time.

MRS. ROSS
I couldn't agree with you more, and we don't **want** the neighborhood to change, do we? Believe me, that's what we're all about. That's what I want, that's what you want, that's what Iris Mayo Teague wants.

> *(ROSETTA enters. MRS. ROSS falls silent as ROSETTA approaches her desk.)*

(To ROSETTA.) Hello, this is the Little City Hall. Were you looking for anyone here?

EILEEN
This is my neighbor, Mrs. Douglas. She lives down the block.

ROSETTA
My name is Rosetta Douglas. I see you're busy with Mrs. Burke. I'll sit down and wait till you're done.

EILEEN
You go ahead. I was just about done anyhow.

> *(Stands.)*

MRS. ROSS
(To ROSETTA.) Why don't you sit down.

> *(Takes EILEEN by the arm and walks a few paces.)*

Could you please wait while I deal with her? I have something to ask you.

EILEEN

(Surprised.) Sure, I'm in no hurry.

> *(Sits in a straight chair against the wall.)*

MRS. ROSS

(Walks behind her desk.) You know we're the Little City Hall, Little with a capital 'L'. We don't work miracles. You have to go downtown for most things ...

ROSETTA

My family been living in this neighborhood for eight years. When we first moved in, we had trouble with some of the teenage boys. My husband contacted the boys' parents and we didn't have no trouble since. But for the last couple weeks, a lot of little things been adding up ... And I think the trouble is starting over. Now we called the police but they haven't done a thing. I came here to see if you can put pressure on them.

MRS. ROSS

Pressure the police? I'm sorry, Rosetta, I don't think we can help you. We have to work **with** the police, not against them.

ROSETTA

I don't want you to work against them. I want you to get them to help me. I want them to send a patrol car in front of my house. Sometimes my son sits up till four in the morning looking out the window. We can't go on living like this.

MRS. ROSS

To tell you the truth, I think it would be more in your interest if we stay out of it. They're just going to feel we're interfering. Each agency is separate. There's the police department, there's the department of public works, there's us, the city hall system –

> *(EILEEN begins to pay full
> attention.)*

ROSETTA

You can still help me. When that sidewalk was broke for
three months in front of the Shanahan's house, they came to
you and you got the department of public works to fix it.
So I'm coming to you to get them to fix that street light in
front of my house. It's pitch black out there at night. It
makes it real easy for those troublemakers. It's bad for the
whole block. Them hanging out there and swearing till all
hours.

MRS. ROSS

Teenage boys are always pulling pranks. Oh, I can agree with
you there, Rosetta, they are a nuisance.

ROSETTA

My wash was spray painted with the word NIGGER.

> *(CURTIS walks in and stands
> quietly by the door. He has
> come to wait for ROSETTA.)*

MRS. ROSS

You know if any of us moved to Roxbury, I'm sure we'd
have plenty of trouble. People like to be with their own
kind. It's human nature, like dogs and cats.

ROSETTA

I know I got a right to my own home, that we fixed up and
made nice. I know my family got a right to the police
protecting us safe as anybody living on our block. Now if
you won't help me, I'm gonna have to go right over your
head.

MRS. ROSS

(Closes her eyes with a knowing smile and with a shake of

her head.) I seem to be talking over your head. You simply don't understand, dear –

ROSETTA
(Slowly.) Don't call me dear, don't call me Rosetta, do not talk down to me!

MRS. ROSS
(Nervous, voice rising, but not yelling.) What do you want me to call you? Your honor? Your excellency? You have a lot of nerve to walk into this office and order me around. Is that how you people think you can get what you want?

> *(ROSETTA stares at her in silence.)*

Why are you staring at me that way?

ROSETTA
You not gonna lift a finger to help me. You gonna sit there on your skinny ass and let my house get painted on, rocks through my front windows, dirty phonecalls in the night, threats and --

MRS. ROSS
I think you better leave, Mrs. Douglas.

ROSETTA
(Starts slowly. Pulls bouse out of her purse and slowly begins to unfurl it and hold it up.) You look at this here blouse. Go on, you look at it. This is the last present my daughter's daddy gave her. And those rotten dirty thieving punks smeared it all over with red paint I can't scrub out and spoiled it for her!

> *(Holds the blouse in front of MRS. ROSS' face.)*

You take this blouse home and you make your daughter wear it! You tell your daughter to put on a blouse that say

NIGGERS SUCK and wear it down to Dudley Station in
Roxbury! You put it on yourself and sit here in it. Go on,
put it on! See how you like it! It sure do fit you to a tee!
You no different from the little shits that did this! Here!

> *(Throws the blouse in her face
> and storms out. EILEEN turns
> toward ROSETTA as if to
> follow her but is frozen.)*

MRS. ROSS

Don't you hit me!

> *(Responds as if slapped.)*

Get out of here! Don't ever let me see you in this office again
or I'll call the police.

> *(ROSETTA walks proudly
> past CURTIS and out into the
> street. He follows. She sobs
> and he embraces her.)*

MRS. ROSS

(To EILEEN.) Did you see what that woman did to me? I
don't believe it. Throwing her dirty laundry in my face!
I should call the police.

EILEEN

(Deeply embarrassed.) You know she's right about the
streetlight.

MRS. ROSS

She threatened my life! She threatened my daughter's life!

EILEEN

(Trying to calm her down.) You were both so mad at each
other.

MRS. ROSS

That's exactly what we're up against, Eileen. Do you see how they try to take over?

> *(Reaches for the phone but doesn't dial.)*

EILEEN

Mrs. Ross, are you all right? I have to go.

MRS. ROSS

(Shaking with anger.) Eileen, you're my witness, you saw what that woman did to me ...

> *(Collecting herself a little.)*

Before you walk out, could you be one of the bus hostesses tomorrow for the senior citizens?

EILEEN

I don't know.

MRS. ROSS

You and Joe are going to the rally anyway, right?

EILEEN

(In a hurry to get out.) I guess so. I don't know what Joe wants to do tomorrow.

> *(Leaves.)*

MRS. ROSS

(Lights dim as she dials and speaks.) Walter? Come on down here and pick me up! I'm shaking. You don't know what just happened to me.

> *(Trails off, lights out.)*

◆ ◆ ◆

scene 6

*A large windowless wall.
MICHAEL, wearing his WHIP
jacket, pastes up posters. As
he sings to himself, lights
slowly rise on SUZANNE who
is slightly in advance of
FRANKLIN and dragging him
along.*

MICHAEL

(Singing.)   *Ninety-four posters of Bitch on the wall,
ninety-four posters of Bitch.
If one of those posters should happen to fall,
ninety-three posters of Bitch on the wall.*

*Ninety-three posters of Bitch on the wall,
ninety-three posters of Bitch ...*

SUZANNE

That's him. Now, isn't he the same punk that ruined our
laundry?

FRANKLIN

The jacket's different, but the pants are the same ... same
build.

SUZANNE

He was wearing a leather jacket when he messed with me. But
it's him.

FRANKLIN

(As SUZANNE runs up to MICHAEL.) You sure?

SUZANNE

Hey, shithead! Where's your friends?

MICHAEL

(Turns, frightened, using his wallpaper brush as a weapon.)
What the hell do you want? Get out of here.

SUZANNE

Outnumbered this time? Why don't you try to put your dirty hands on me now like you did Wednesday?

MICHAEL

(To FRANKLIN.) She's crazy. What's she talking about?

SUZANNE

What happened to your jacket with the paint on it? Did you wear it when you painted NIGGER on our door yesterday? WHIP, huh.

> *(She steps close to read the insignia.)*

Somebody gonna whip you.

MICHAEL

(Brandishes the brush at SUZANNE.) Stay back, you crazy bitch.

FRANKLIN

Just calm down, kid. We're here to warn you, loud and clear. You keep your hands off my sister or I'll stuff that brush down your throat.

MICHAEL

I'm not scared of you. Filthy niggers!

> *(Walking away.)*

Go back to Roxbury where you belong.

SUZANNE

(Pushes him hard against the wall. He's surprised.) You know where we belong. You know real well where we live. You hang out under our streetlight all night.

FRANKLIN

Listen to me, boy, and you listen good. I don't want you ever

calling up my Mama to talk dirty. Don't you be throwing
paint at our house. This is your last and only warning. You
real brave on the end of a telephone cord. But you shaking
right now.

MICHAEL
You better watch out from now on. If me and my friends
see you walking in the street, you're dead.

FRANKLIN
Any friends you want to bring along to fight for you, we'll
wipe up the street with them.

MICHAEL
We got an organization now. We know how to take care of
you people.

> *(Draws himself up.)*

You're gonna find out what this uniform means.

FRANKLIN
*(Puts one hand in his pocket and the other slowly on
MICHAEL's shoulder, freezing him. He is playing macho.)*
We don't see no reason to stand here prolonging this chit-chat,
much as we do admire your new bright blue little league
jacket. We're not gonna touch one greasy hair on your bone
head -- yet. If you ever bother my sister, if you ever call up
my Mama, if you ever come near my house again, I'm gonna
beat you purple as a grape.

> *(Takes his hand off.*
> *MICHAEL runs.)*

SUZANNE
Look at him run! I knew they were just punks with no more
guts than to sneak around in the yard. If we see him by our
house again, let's get him, Franklin.

> *(Puts her arm through*
> *FRANKLIN's rigid arm.)*

FRANKLIN

Why we always got to fight these punks for every damn thing?
I feel like giving up and moving out of this damn neighborhood
... But I wouldn't give them the satisfaction.

> *(SUZANNE keeps her arm*
> *linked through his and begins*
> *to tow him off. He goes along*
> *stiffly but willingly.)*

◆ ◆ ◆

scene 7

Sculley's Jack of Diamonds
Bar. Saturday afternoon around
5:00. Keith slouches over the
bar. He's been there for an
hour and is beginning to get
drunk. The afternoon crowd
having thinned out, PETER
stands behind the bar talking
with KEITH. JOE stands to
the side, playing darts by
himself.

PETER

Don't worry about it. You did the right thing, believe me.

KEITH

When Suzanne opened the door I said, 'Come on, kids, we're
leaving.' ... Then I turned around. 'If I ever see you with my
children again, I'll file kidnapping charges.'

PETER

I bet your wife loved that.

KEITH

To tell you the truth, I don't give a shit.

PETER

(Wanting to enjoy GINA's reaction.) Go on, what did she say?

KEITH

She was still at work. I left the kids with my mother ... Give me another.

PETER

(As he goes to get the drink.) You did it for their own good. That Douglas woman is a maniac. How do you know what that woman might do to your kids, after what happened down at Little City Hall today?

KEITH

(As PETER brings him the drink.) What are you talking about?

PETER

Remember Mrs. Ross? She's about five feet tall, right? She's sitting there by her desk calling up the old age homes, I saw her myself not fifteen minutes before, when that Douglas woman come charging in there this morning demanding to have some kid arrested who busted their window. Stupid ape thinks it's the police department. When Mrs. Ross says she can't do a thing, the woman goes crazy.

> *(JOE having overheard bits of the conversation at the dartboard, comes over to listen. He takes with him a wrapped gift and sets it down*

*on the bar. PETER continues,
conscious now of spinning a
tale for two.)*

Says she'll get Mrs. Ross fired. Then when Mrs. Ross laughs
in her face, the ape says she's going to have a bunch of guys
from Roxbury beat up on her daughter Darlene.

JOE

What's Darlene got to do with it? She's such a pretty little
thing.

PETER

Then she takes out a dirty old tee shirt she had in her bag and
slaps Mrs. Ross right in the face with it. Can you picture it,
that little grey-haired lady sitting there and that big ape
screaming.

(Imitates.)

'You nothing but white trash. You all trying to get me!'

JOE

Why don't they mind their own business, that's what I don't
understand. You know, one or two families, people don't like
it, but we leave them alone. Then they go and start making
trouble ... What time is it? I got to be going.

*(Doesn't move. Clearly not
about to.)*

KEITH

Nobody's going to want to move down here if they have to be
scared for their kids. Renovating this block is a pipe dream if
this garbage keeps happening.

PETER

That's what Sculley's always saying: 'The guy who cleans up
this neighborhood, cleans up.' There's a lot of money to be
made here.

KEITH

I've got ideas I haven't even laid out to my Dad yet. We're nine minutes away from the center of the city by subway. We could pick up a couple of those run-down triple-deckers around the corner for a song and put up high rises. Attract a whole other class of people ... Only my stupid old lady is on my back about moving all the time ... I never should've married her.

PETER

Listen to your mother next time.

> *(Reaches under the bar and hands KEITH a pamphlet.)*

She's making trouble for everybody. Look at this garbage she's handing out.

KEITH

She's still wearing jeans, for Christ sake. She's holding me back, and I'm sick of it.

> *(Starts to look at the pamphlet.)*

I'm gonna leave her.

JOE

Where are you gonna leave her, in your mother's house?

KEITH

(Glares at JOE, angry. Reads aloud from the pamphlet.) 'Your children's education is at stake. While greedy politicians have you fighting Black against white, the schools are getting worse!'

> *(To PETER.)*

Where did you get this drivel?

PETER

Where do you think? From your wife and that parent's group of hers. Listen to me, get hold of Neil Hagstrom. He took good care of me when Peggy Dawley tried to slap me with that paternity suit.

KEITH
She's not getting the kids. My mother'll take care of them.

PETER
Believe me, when Hagstrom gets done with her, she'll be lucky to walk out with clothes on her back.

JOE
(As he realizes KEITH is serious, tries to put his arm around KEITH, who freezes.) You don't want to walk out just because of a few bad scenes. Some weeks it's the Saturday night fights every night. But a lot of times you know we come home with the whole world on our shoulders, and it don't really have a lot to do with them ... But it don't have to be like that, going downhill. You can do something about it.

(Shows him the package.)

For Eileen's birthday. You got to give them a little something now and again. 'Once in every week, Draino in every drain.'

KEITH
You're a real fucking philosopher, aren't you, Joe?

(MICHAEL enters. Stands at the end of the bar, staring at PETER till he catches PETER's eye.)

MICHAEL
(To PETER.) I got to talk to you.

(The men turn their heads at first, but then ignore him.)

PETER
(Saunters toward him.) What do you want, a beer?

JOE

(To KEITH.) Sometimes you just have to ride out the bad times in a marriage. Maybe one of you don't feel like it sometimes ... Don't give up, stick it out.

PETER

(From down the bar.) There's another job for you, Joe. Marriage Counselor. Leave the guy alone.

JOE

(Trying to get KEITH alone to talk.) Come on, and I'll teach you how to throw darts.

KEITH

You couldn't teach me how to throw farts.

JOE

(Determined not to feel insulted by a drunk.) A dollar says I can beat you.

KEITH

Jesus, you're like a nagging woman. All right, all right, you start. I'll be there in a minute.

> *(Calls to PETER as JOE goes to the dartboard and starts to throw.)*

Another of the same.

PETER

(Engrossed in an inaudible conversation with MICHAEL, who tells about the confrontation in the previous scene.) Half a minute.

JOE

(Stands in front of the dartboard, carefully aiming his shots. He throws one: Close to dead center.) Look at that. Haven't lost my eye in ten years.

> *(As JOE throws the next one,
> KEITH lumbers, sodden, to the
> board. Falls in a chair near
> JOE.)*

Not so good. Like I was saying, you got to keep trying.

KEITH
(To PETER.) Where the hell is that drink? I thought this was a bar. Not much of a bar, but a bar.

JOE
(Throws another dart.) Not bad, not bad.

> *(Walks over to collect the darts.)*

PETER
(Strides over, followed by MICHAEL. To KEITH.) We been challenged. Bunch of niggers led by Franklin Douglas just cornered my brother. Said they're going to match us man for man.

> *(JOE hands the darts to KEITH.)*

KEITH
(Takes the darts. Sits there too drunk to move.) Kill 'em all.
> *(To MICHAEL.)*

What are you going to do?

MICHAEL
(Points to his WHIP emblem.) That's what this is all about.

PETER
Anybody with any guts around here is going to fight. We're ready for them.

JOE
(To KEITH.) You playing or not? I told you I got to be going soon.

MICHAEL

(*Ignores JOE.*) He said he was warning me loud and clear. He said that any white that goes anywhere near his house is gonna be beat purple as a grape. No nigger is going to tell me where I can and can't go. Tonight we'll see who can go near their house. And not just me ... all the guys from WHIP.

JOE

(*Trying to pull KEITH to his feet.*) Come back to the dartboard. Take your turn. I want to talk to you. Keith, there's never been a divorce in our family.

PETER

Shut up about your darts. We're talking about our constitutional rights being violated, and you want to play darts.

JOE

I'm trying to talk to my cousin about something important.

KEITH

(*Slurring speech.*) Hey, cousin Joe, I didn't say I don't want to play.

> (*Throws a dart at JOE's feet.*
> *JOE jumps away, annoyed.*)

Let's dance, Joe.

> (*Throws another. Angry, JOE*
> *jumps to avoid it.*)

PETER

Make him do the hustle.

JOE

Grown up idiots! You're as crazy as the kids. Grown up idiots!

> (*Begins to storm out.*)

PETER

(Before JOE leaves.) Hey, don't forget your birthday present.

> *(Humiliated, JOE must pass all to retrieve the present. They are silently glowering at him until KEITH begins to sing.)*

KEITH

Happy Birthday to you,
Happy Birthday to you ...

MICHAEL

> *(Lights a book of matches and holds it like a birthday cake covered with candles to JOE, as JOE comes to get the present.)*

Make a wish, Two-Beer!

KEITH, MICHAEL, PETER

Happy Birthday, dear Eileen,
Happy Birthday to you.

> *(JOE rushes out furious. They all laugh outrageously as the lights dim.)*

◆ ◆ ◆

scene 8

The kitchen of the BURKE family, around 7:30 PM Saturday. The scene opens in the dark with TERRY bringing out the birthday cake, candles lit. The first voices are those of TERRY and JOE singing HAPPY BIRTHDAY TO YOU. As the song ends, EILEEN blows out the candles and the lights come up. They are all seated at the table. The table is set with their best dishes and a tablecloth. A bottle of red wine and flowers are on the table. EILEEN wears her fanciest dress, a little tight.

EILEEN

(Delighted.) If Cathy would call, this would be a perfect birthday.

TERRY

Except for the presents.

EILEEN

(Tries to give him a hug that he resists stiffly.) Tee, don't be silly. I love having two purses. I'll be the best dressed woman in the office.

JOE

That was great lasagna. I don't know what's wrong with Keith. Gina's a real good cook.

EILEEN

Don't you think it was better than we could get in any restaurant? Lots of cheese and sausage, and the sauce ...

JOE
Yeah, but next year I'm taking you out again to the Villa Rosa.

EILEEN
(To TERRY.) That's where your father took me the second time we went out. It was July and he brought me a rose he said was the color of my hair. Remember, Joe, it was raining so hard we sat in the car for half an hour waiting for it to stop --

TERRY
You told me that story a hundred times.

> *(A pause. TERRY has stopped conversation.)*

What time is it? I got to go.

JOE
On your mother's birthday, you can stay home for once.

TERRY
Aw, it's Saturday night. I'll stay home tomorrow.

> *(From now on he is preparing to leave. He doesn't look at them when they speak to him and he never interrupts his preparations.)*

EILEEN
Do you have to leave right now? Have another piece of cake.

TERRY
I'm going to the movies with Michael, and I'm late.

> *(Walks into the living room. He tears open a bag, puts on the new WHIP jacket, and*

*preens before a small mirror
he obviously wishes were
larger.)*

EILEEN

(Calls into him.) What are you going to see?

(TERRY doesn't answer.)

Terry, you're not going to see one of those X-rated movies, are you?

JOE

If he is, maybe I'll go.

EILEEN

Joe! He'll hear you. Don't encourage him.

JOE

Aw, there's nothing they could have in those movies I didn't see in Hamburg when I was in the Army.

EILEEN

(As he goes out the door.) Where did you get that jacket?

TERRY

(Leaving.) It's for a club. A lot of the guys have them. See you.

EILEEN

(Serious.) Do you think he's really going to see one of those movies? That Michael ... I just don't like Terry hanging out with him.

JOE

Terry follows that jackass around like a fish after the bait.

EILEEN

(Pause.) We're losing him, Joe.

(Gets up and starts to clear the table.)

JOE

You got to let go of him. He's not your little boy any more.

EILEEN

(Stops clearing the table.) When was the last time Cathy called? We lost her, we're losing Terry. And I don't know what we have left with each other.

(Sits at the table.)

It's just not the same between us.

JOE

We don't do so bad. Lots of husbands and wives, they're throwing the furniture at each other. Breaking up over nothing.

EILEEN

We used to talk sometimes, Joe. You don't trust me no more. I can't say anything to you without you accusing me of thinking you're a bum.

JOE

You don't treat me so special. Sometimes you make me feel like I don't even belong here when you and Terry are having one of your private talks. It's like you say to him, 'Quick, shh, here comes your old man.'

EILEEN

I just think we've lost him. I used to be so proud of how he never lied to me. Now he lies all the time.

JOE

Terry! Terry! Terry! That's all you think about. Sure he lies. He never was the altar boy you thought he was. He was lying tonight.

EILEEN

Then he was going to a dirty movie.

JOE

If he's out with Michael tonight, he's not going to any movie. Today at the Jack, Michael was talking about doing something to those coloreds down the block. There's going to be trouble over there tonight ... Something out there's making all the kids crazy.

EILEEN

It's something in here too, Joe. The way you talk about Blacks. You make like it's okay to blame everything on them. Not getting a job. Taxes going up.

JOE

Whose fault is it, what's happening in this neighborhood? Rosetta Douglas threatened to bring in a bunch of Blacks from Roxbury to beat up on Mrs. Ross' pretty little girl Darlene.

EILEEN

Where did you hear that?

JOE

At the Jack. It happened in Little City Hall this morning. Rosetta Douglas came charging in there and slapped Mrs. Ross right in the face with an old dirty rag. It's all over the neighborhood. Everybody was talking about it at Sculley's, and when I stopped at the liquor store to get the wine, they were talking about it there too.

EILEEN

(Snaps at him.) She didn't do that! I was there this morning.

JOE

So was Peter, and I heard the story straight from him.

EILEEN

He walked out of there before the whole thing happened. Rosetta Douglas came to see if they would fix the street light on our block. Is that so bad?

JOE

Half the neighborhood is up in arms. And those guys with the jackets are gonna run them out of the neighborhood tonight.

EILEEN

(Stands up.) I'm gonna call the police.

JOE

On your own son?

(Pause.)

EILEEN

That woman didn't do anything wrong.

JOE

You think it's just Terry and Michael and a bunch of other little blockheads. It's Peter Thibault and Jack Sculley and god knows who else is behind them. Eileen, if you do anything, the same thing is going to happen to us.

EILEEN

(After a silence, picks up the phonebook and looks for a number.) I'm not calling the police, Joe. I'll just tell Mrs. Douglas. I won't give my name.
(Dials.)

JOE

(Nervous.) I don't see what you're getting yourself mixed up in this for.

EILEEN

It's busy.

(Hangs up. Pauses. Silence as neither knows what to say. She dials again.)

Still busy.

JOE

(Angry.) What do you got to drag us into this for?

EILEEN

Joe Burke, what is the matter with you?

(Dials again. Hangs up.)

Still busy. Gina said something about them getting dirty phonecalls. I wonder if they have the phone off the hook.

JOE

It's their own fault then. You tried, right?

EILEEN

I'll go down the block and tell them.

JOE

You're crazy. You're going over there alone?

EILEEN

Come with me, Joe. We'll just tell them and leave. We don't have to go inside.

JOE

I wouldn't get the time of day from any guy in this neighborhood. Come on, there's still some wine. Forget it. You're going to get hurt.

EILEEN

(Puts her coat on.) I'll be back in five minutes, I promise. I'll be back and we'll forget about it and we'll have a nice night. I just got to do it.

JOE

What's wrong with you? You want to get us mixed up in this trouble? Sit down, Eileen. You don't know what you're doing!

EILEEN

Joe, come with me. I'd be so proud of you.

> *(EILEEN stands at the door staring at JOE's back, hoping he will come. JOE sits, silent and withdrawn, his back rigid. There is a pause as every one of his senses anticipates EILEEN's next move. She leaves. Hearing the door shut, he sits motionless, almost without breathing. Automatically his hand grabs the fork and he eats, pausing to chew and stare at the table. He picks up the lasagna and the birthday cake. Suddenly he stops eating and throws down his fork. He sits as if paralyzed. Then he pushes the table away and gets up. Staring at nothing and swaying slightly, he stands over the table. With a loud moan of anger, he seizes the tablecloth and sweeps it off, dishes, wine bottle and cutlery, throwing it to the floor.)*

◆ ◆ ◆

scene 9

*The living room of the
DOUGLAS family. Saturday
evening, immediately following
the previous scene. ROSETTA
is wearing a long dress in a bright
and dramatic print, her hair worn
in a dressier manner than usual.
CURTIS is also dressed to step
out. SUZANNE is wearing her
street clothes as she tries to
usher them out the door.*

SUZANNE

*(Stands by the door, attempting literally to push her mother
out.)* Mama, go! It's been years since you wore that dress. You
look so fine, don't spoil your big evening. Curtis, make her go!

CURTIS

Who is that woman who called? You trust her?

ROSETTA

(Stands immobile, frowning with uncertainty.) Gina. She
white but she always been my friend. I trust she heard
something going on. About now I don't put nothing past the
people around here.

SUZANNE

Mama, nothing's gonna happen here tonight that doesn't happen
to me every single day in school. Go on now. They're just a
bunch of cowards.

ROSETTA

Curtis, you go ahead. It's your own sister's party. Everybody
be so disappointed.

CURTIS

They seen me a thousand times. It's you they're waiting to size
up.

ROSETTA

I'm not leaving my house and I'm not leaving my child.

SUZANNE

I'm no child any more, Mama. So don't treat me like a child.

CURTIS

The two of you, stop picking on each other. Aint no time to be bickering. I'm not walking out of here without you, Rosetta ... I wish they'd show their faces now. I'd rub them in the concrete.

> *(EILEEN has been staring at the house for the last few minutes. She now comes out of the shadows to the door.)*

ROSETTA

Maybe when Franklin gets home from work, we can go ... How about that?

> *(EILEEN knocks. SUZANNE runs to the window. CURTIS grabs a baseball bat from the corner.)*

SUZANNE

It's that woman from down the street. The one you said was in the Little City Hall this morning.

ROSETTA

(Walking to the door. CURTIS follows her.) Now what in hell she want?

CURTIS

Anyone with her?

> *(ROSETTA opens the door.)*

SUZANNE

Not a soul on the street but her.

EILEEN

(To ROSETTA.) I'm awful sorry to bother you. I'm not here to visit.

ROSETTA

After eight years I didn't figure it was the Welcome Wagon.

SUZANNE

(Purposely so as to be heard by EILEEN.) What does she want?

EILEEN

I'm sorry ... My husband was down at that bar, the Jack, and he heard some people talking. There's going to be trouble here tonight.

CURTIS

(Behind ROSETTA.) Exactly what kind of trouble are you talking about?

EILEEN

(To ROSETTA.) All I know is a lot of guys at the bar were talking about how you threatened Darlene Ross.

ROSETTA

Darlene Ross? I thought that scarecrow's name was **Pauline** Ross.

CURTIS

(Calm but angry.) I don't understand what you want here.

SUZANNE

Don't trust that woman, Mama. Her son and another punk gave me a hard time Wednesday.

ROSETTA

(To SUZANNE.) You didn't tell me nothing about a hard time.

SUZANNE

They tried to jump me in the street.

EILEEN

(Walks in. To SUZANNE.) Terry Burke? He wouldn't do that!

> *(ROSETTA closes the door behind her.)*

SUZANNE

I know who he is. Don't look at me like you think he's some kind of angel.

ROSETTA

(Stern.) Why is this the first time I'm hearing about this?

EILEEN

But Terry would never --

CURTIS

What did those white boys do to you?

ROSETTA

Answer us, Suzanne. What happened?

SUZANNE

Wednesday afternoon, I was coming home from school, when they wouldn't let me by. They started saying these disgusting things. Michael tried to grab me here.

> *(Points awkwardly to her breast.)*

Then I hit him with my books and ran.

> *(GINA knocks. Everybody freezes.)*

ROSETTA

(Goes to look out the window.) It's Gina.

EILEEN
But what did Terry do?

SUZANNE
Stood there laughing.

> *(She moves to stand near CURTIS.)*

GINA
(Goes past ROSETTA, looking very upset and paces. She has been crying.) Everything all right so far? Saw a lot of kids drinking beer down in the park ... Eileen, what are you doing here?

EILEEN
(In an almost inaudible, sad voice.) Joe was in the bar and told me about this rumor flying around.

ROSETTA
(To GINA.) Police say they won't come unless something happens ... *(To EILEEN.)* I appreciate your telling me about the lie going around, Mrs. Burke, but what the hell good that do me? If those punks come with rocks, what can I do?

> *(Acts out herself making a speech.)*

'Hello there, neighbors and punks. Now sit down quiet on the lawn while I tell you the real lowdown on what happened at Little City Hall.'

GINA
Look, I'm staying. But they won't listen to me either.

> *(After a long pause, to EILEEN.)*

Eileen?

EILEEN

I can't! I promised Joe I'd be back in five minutes ... It's my birthday.

ROSETTA

(A long knowing look at CURTIS.) Uh huh.

GINA

Eileen, please stay! It's a white neighborhood. They're outnumbered. The only way to stop this trouble is if whites in the neighborhood stand up to those punks too.

EILEEN

Those punks is my son!

CURTIS

Are we talking about a couple of snotnosed kids with spray paint cans, or what?

GINA

Keith came home plastered and I didn't understand everything he said. He kept talking about 'Tonight we go to war. All the guys from WHIP. All the guys from WHIP.'

CURTIS

Rosetta, come here.

> *(She comes to him where he*
> *stands with SUZANNE by the*
> *window looking out.)*

For your own good, baby, we can't pussyfoot around with these people no more. I been holding my tongue. But we need help and we can't count on nobody here. I want you to tell me it's all right to call up my sister and get some brothers from the party to come on over.

ROSETTA

Those people don't live here. What about when they go

home? I don't want a stupid rumor about a blouse to start a race war. Me and my kids still got to live here.

GINA
(Comes over.) It's not just a rumor about a blouse. People are excited about a gang of Blacks beating up Michael Thibault this afternoon.

SUZANNE
It was just me and Franklin, and we didn't beat him up. We just told him he better stay away from our house.

ROSETTA
What did you go and do that for? You know these people are crazy. Why give them an excuse?

SUZANNE
Mama, I'm sick of you getting mad at us for fighting back. What do you want us to do, pray while they throw rocks at the house?

CURTIS
(To ROSETTA.) You know what the trouble with you is? You want to protect everybody yourself. This here is a strong young woman. She don't want her Mama to fight her battles.

ROSETTA
(Upset. Turns away. She and EILEEN catch each other's gaze in silence.) You don't know what you gonna do with them any more.

EILEEN
You try to tell them for their own good, but they just go and do what they want, and you don't even know.

ROSETTA
(Turning back to SUZANNE.) This was your big idea. Now how's your brother gonna get home tonight? They're gonna

lie in wait for him where he gets off the bus ... Curtis, would you go on down to the Oyster House and pick up Franklin? Please.

CURTIS

I'm not leaving you here to face some mob.

ROSETTA

I don't want that boy coming home from the bus and walking into a fight or an ambush. They're gonna be out to get him.

GINA

There may be other people coming. I stopped by the Shanahans. They were out but I left a message with their babysitter.

CURTIS

Great. The Ku Klux Klan is marching on the house and we're waiting for the Shanahans to pick up their messages.

EILEEN

(Sits down hard, suddenly on the couch.) Well, I'll stay! I don't know what good I'll be able to do, but I'll stay.

SUZANNE

I'm not scared. I'd rather die than be scared all the time.

GINA

Well, I'm not ashamed to say I'm scared. I don't like getting dirty phone calls in the night any better than you do ...

> *(She sits on the couch next to EILEEN.)*

Keith told me tonight he wants to leave me and take away my kids.

EILEEN

He's not serious.

> *(GINA starts to cry into her
> hands. She tries to hold back
> but can't.)*

ROSETTA
Nothing's happening yet, Curtis. You got plenty of time to fetch him and get back.

CURTIS
(Looks uncomfortable at GINA weeping.) Okay. But if I see anybody out front when I get back, I'll park down the block and come in the side door. I'll be back fast as I can.

> *(SUZANNE sits on GINA's
> other side and takes her hand.)*

ROSETTA
(Escorts him to the door, puts her arm in his. Softly, to him only.) Yeah, I remember you told me what a fast worker you were ...

> *(CURTIS touches her face.
> Leaves.)*

EILEEN
But if he was drunk, he was just shooting off his mouth.

GINA
He says he's going to see some lawyer named Hagstrom. He's going to divorce me and take my children away.

ROSETTA
(Sits down in the easy chair.) You hold on to those kids, Gina. He go to see a lawyer, you go to see a lawyer too.

EILEEN
Does he have another woman?

GINA

I've never seen him like he was tonight. He was drunk and crazy. Look at my arm.

(Shows them bruises.)

ROSETTA

Check him out in the morning. See if it was just the bottle talking, or if he means it. If he's serious, you take those kids to your mother's. Tomorrow.

GINA

(Stops crying. Gets control of herself.) I feel like Keith has gone over to the other side. They're getting rid of me and he's helping.

EILEEN

There's Cathy's room. Gina, up in the dormer away from us ... I can't promise nothing ... Really, it's up to Joe.

GINA

Maybe ... You haven't lived with little kids in a long time.

(To SUZANNE.)

I'm so sorry about Keith dragging the kids out today ... Was he ... real ugly to you?

ROSETTA

(To EILEEN.) Well, whatever they do, they're not gonna throw snowballs. Why don't you take off your coat?

EILEEN

(Takes it off. Looks around at the room. Through this whole scene one or another of the women are constantly looking out the window.) You sure have done a lot with this house. I remember what a mess it was when the last people lived here.

ROSETTA

(Mixture of pride and apology.) We were lucky to get this

house in the first place. Banks'll only give you a mortgage in
some areas. We were gonna knock that wall down to make a
great big living room.

SUZANNE

When we first moved in, I was only eight, but I remember
some punk throwing a rock through our front window. Then
Daddy went and put in a picture window three times as big.

ROSETTA

Suzanne, why don't you put on a pot of coffee. And see if
there's any of those cookies left.

SUZANNE

(Gets up.) Sure.

GINA

(Follows her into the kitchen.) Suzanne, you know the
children love you. They don't know what's going on and they
cried half the afternoon.

EILEEN

(After a silence.) But do you mind telling me why you want
to live here? It must be hard on you to stay.

ROSETTA

Hard was where we lived before ... Well, I'll tell you, Mrs.
Burke, we only move into white neighborhoods to bug
whites. Actually we all love dead dogs on the stoop and
junkies nodding out on the corner, and we love having our
kids go to overcrowded garbage heap schools, with teachers so
old they shaking all the time. And we love having our kids
hang around streets where half the men are out of work.
And we love living two bus rides from the subway ... But
we put up with all the inconveniences of neighborhoods
where they pick up the garbage and clean the streets just
'cause we love to bring property values down.

EILEEN

You must hate us so much.

ROSETTA

I'm sorry, but can't you see, this is my house just like that's your house. My husband died in this house when his heart failed, just burned up with frustration, I think. He was only thirty-seven.

EILEEN

(Struck by that.) Younger than my Joe ... I never came into your house for eight years. I guess I never thought we'd have anything to say to each other.

ROSETTA

Don't brood on it. You here now ...

> *(Far off sounds of mayhem, confused yet rhythmic. At first it could be no more than a disturbance next door (or in the lobby of the theater), a crash that doesn't concern us. The rumble grows louder. EILEEN and ROSETTA freeze.)*

GINA

(Entering from the kitchen.) Listen. Do you hear it?

> *(Almost immediately the sounds become distinguishable. A crowd of teenagers and men carrying bats, bottles, ax handles, rocks or tire irons move in close packs to gather in front of the house. Some slurring their*

*words, all screaming to be heard
above the others they chant,
NIGGERS OUT ... NIGGERS
OUT. Leading the pack is
MICHAEL, followed by
TERRY who is carrying a
megaphone. MICHAEL and
TERRY wear their WHIP
jackets as do some but not all
of the others.*

*SUZANNE, ROSETTA, GINA
and EILEEN rush to the
windows.)*

SUZANNE

See those cowards! Looks like some softball team for all the
half wits in this town. Michael Thibault, Terry Burke, Vincent
Drago from school, Mr. Murphy ...

CROWD

Come on out and fight, niggers!
Get out of this neighborhood! Go back to Africa!
Troublemakers!
Fuck you, niggers!

ROSETTA

There's grown men out there. I'm calling the police.

(Runs to the phone.)

EILEEN

Terry!

(To herself.)

It is Terry ...

*(At the far end of the stage,
barely visible in the shadows we*

> *see JOE, watching, not a part
> of the crowd. His hands are in
> his pockets.)*

GINA

Stay away from the windows! We better turn down the lights.

> *(The lights dim, as if lamps are
> turned down. ROSETTA is
> arguing with the police, trying
> to get them to come despite
> their protests that nothing
> illegal has yet happened. She
> stands back near the door to
> the kitchen.*
>
> *GINA and SUZANNE are
> crouched by the windows.
> EILEEN stands transfixed
> staring at TERRY.)*

EILEEN

(To herself.) He doesn't know what he's doing.

> *(As the catcalls continue, some
> men in the crowd start throwing
> rocks against the house.)*

MICHAEL

(To TERRY.) Go on, do it. Now's your chance. Make your
speech. You wanted to carry the goddamn thing, so do it.

TERRY

(Hesitantly raising the megaphone to his mouth.) Get out!
> *(Again hesitantly.)*

Get out of this neighborhood!

> *(Catcalls from the crowd follow
> each of his phrases. It is clear*

*that each statement makes him
feel good enough to continue.)*

I've lived in this neighborhood for all of my life and I'm here
to say NIGGERS GET OUT!

*(EILEEN rushes out of the
house.)*

GINA
Don't, Eileen. Where are you going?

EILEEN
(On the steps, to the crowd.) What are you doing? Have you
all gone crazy?

*(TERRY lowers the megaphone
from his mouth.)*

MICHAEL
(To EILEEN.) Shut up, let him talk.

TERRY
(To MICHAEL.) I didn't know she was going to be here.

MICHAEL
It's on your own block, you asshole! What did you think, she
wasn't gonna hear you? You wanted to be the big man. Now
make your speech, come on.

TERRY
(Hesitates. Fumbles with a piece of paper. Starts to read.) I
have lived on this block my whole life ...

EILEEN
Terry, what are you doing?

*(GINA comes out of the house
and stands next to EILEEN.*

> *TERRY is torn between*
> *MICHAEL and his mother.*
> *Glances from one to the other*
> *and then stares at his paper.)*

TERRY

... And I know how it was before the niggers moved in! I want you people who live on this block to hear me because I know you are afraid to speak out. Well, we don't have to be scared now!

> *(Wild cheers from the crowd.)*

EILEEN

Terry, stop it!

> *(She speaks to the crowd.)*

It's all a lie. What you heard happened at the Little City Hall this morning is all a lie. I was there!

A MEMBER OF THE CROWD

Eileen Burke, get out of here! We don't want to hear it.

GINA

What did these people ever do to you? Listen to her. All of you, listen to her. She's the only one making sense.

> *(As JOE stands on the side of*
> *the stage, watching, PETER*
> *comes up to him.)*

TERRY

(Continues to read, fumbling with the text.) We are here tonight not to do violence, but if ... provoked ... we are not afraid. We are here to serve an *(has difficulty with the word)* eviction notice that we want them out.

EILEEN

(Loud. Trying to out-yell the crowd, which is responding

wildly to TERRY's last remark.) Rosetta Douglas didn't do nothing to Darlene. She never said a thing about her! I was there.

MICHAEL
(To EILEEN.) Aw, fuck you. Come on, Terry. They love it!

GINA
Michael Thibault, you don't even live on this block. You're just causing trouble tonight like you always cause trouble. Why should anybody here trust you?

> *(JOE starts for the porch.*
> *PETER holds him back.)*

PETER
The women are all on the rag -- they're crazy. Your kid's okay. He's got guts, that kid. Why don't you go get her out of there, Joe?

> *(JOE stands immobile.)*

TERRY
(As TERRY continues to read, ROSETTA and SUZANNE appear in the doorway, ROSETTA carrying a baseball bat.) We students are sick of what the schools have become ... They are not the same since bussing brought outsiders in here. It used to be OUR school and OUR block before they came ...

EILEEN
(To the crowd, pleading.) You know they called the police. Who do you think is gonna get in trouble?

GINA
You think Michael Thibault and his brother Peter are going to jail? It's you ... They're using all of you!

> *(FRANKLIN and CURTIS make*
> *their way carefully to the house*

along the outskirts of the crowd.
Each carries something that can
be used as a weapon.)

MICHAEL
I'm warning you now, shut up!

(ROSETTA comes forward and
stands next to EILEEN.)

TERRY
(Continues to read.) Now we are no longer alone. There is an
organization of concerned citizens like you and I. It is called
WHIP – White Homeowners ... in....

(Has trouble with pronunciation.)

in ... Pa ... Patriotism.

MICHAEL
(Madly screaming.) WHIP! WHIP!

EILEEN
Michael Thibault, you're a liar. It wasn't no gang of kids from
Roxbury threatened you today.

SUZANNE
(Steps forward.) It was me and Franklin. And you were
scared too!

TERRY
(Leads the crowd in a chant.) We want them out! We want
them out!

(A rock strikes SUZANNE in the
head. She falls. ROSETTA
rushes to SUZANNE and goes
down on her knees beside her.)

EILEEN

(To the crowd in reaction to SUZANNE's assault.) Is that what you're all here for? To protect that lying coward Michael Thibault from a sixteen-year-old girl?

MICHAEL

(As he rushes up on the porch.) I don't care whose goddamn mother you are. You shut your face!

> *(Knocks EILEEN off her feet. EILEEN grabs his shirt, and a scuffle begins. JOE jumps onto the porch and pushes MICHAEL away from EILEEN. At this moment, FRANKLIN grabs the megaphone from TERRY. Someone in the crowd immediately hits him from behind. CURTIS pushes the attacker off FRANKLIN, who is still clutching the megaphone. A couple of people grab FRANKLIN's clothes as CURTIS and FRANKLIN jump for the porch. CURTIS makes it, only to turn and see FRANKLIN being held by one of the men and beaten by MICHAEL. GINA gets SUZANNE to her feet and pulls her back toward the door. ROSETTA, swinging a baseball bat, thwarts the attack on FRANKLIN. As she swings the bat, the crowd steps back, MICHAEL shrinking with them. FRANKLIN, beaten, his*

*clothing torn, drags himself onto
the porch still grasping the
megaphone.*

ROSETTA

Get the hell off my property! Get the hell away from my house!
Any of you take one step closer, I'm gonna split your head in
two!

TERRY

Give us that megaphone back, nigger!

EILEEN

Talk to Terry, Joe. Tell him to go home!

JOE

(Facing the crowd.) Go on home, all of you. What did these
people do to you?

PETER

(Trying to rally the crowd around him.) Two-Beer Burke, the
hero. Can't even hold a job. You gonna hold a crowd back?
Your son's got more guts than you do.

JOE

Yeah, he's only scared of you. I'm not. I lived in this
neighborhood my whole life.

PETER

You're gonna die here, Joe.

JOE

You don't scare me one bit. I've seen scum like you go by
like shit floating down a river. You turn this neighborhood
into a sewer.

(To the crowd.)

These people have been living here for eight years. I didn't

like it neither when they moved in, but they never hurt any
of you.

MICHAEL

Nigger loving faggot!

EILEEN

Don't you say that to him! He's better than all of you.

JOE

I'm not living on a block where any family's pushed out, and
I'm not moving either. You know what that means? I'll be
here every night with these people fighting every goddamn one
of you who shows your face. And that goes for my own son
too.

> *(Looks at TERRY. Police
> sirens approach from a distance.)*

PETER

(Grabs TERRY's arm.) Listen, man, you did good tonight.
You got a bed with us whenever you need it. Go home with
my brother.

> *(Turns to JOE.)*

And you, Joe Burke, don't be coming down to the Jack no
more! Every night in your honor I'm going to pour two beers
down the toilet. Nobody around here's gonna forget this.

> *(To MICHAEL.)*

Come on, let's get out of here.

MICHAEL

(To the crowd.) Let's move it out. We served our notice. We
don't want to get busted before the rally. Tomorrow WHIP
meets again.

> *(Sirens rising. The crowd begins
> to disperse, with MICHAEL*

leading them off. TERRY
doesn't move. Stares at the
ground. JOE stares at TERRY.)

PETER
(To FRANKLIN.) We don't get that megaphone back, nigger, we'll see you in court. Assault and theft. And we're pressing charges.

FRANKLIN
You come up here and get it!

ROSETTA
(Takes megaphone from FRANKLIN and speaks through it.) Press charges against **me**. Rosetta Douglas.

(Says rest of speech without
megaphone.)

I got your megaphone. Know what I'm doing with it? Everytime one of you punks comes lurking outside my door at night I'm going to tell it to the block. I'm broadcasting it.

(PETER motions to TERRY.
Starts to walk off.)

JOE
What are you going to do, Terry?

(TERRY continues to stare at
the ground.)

Come home with your mother and me.

(Walks toward TERRY.
PETER pauses at the edge of
the stage and turns to watch.)

TERRY
You're a loser! ... Peter's right, you're a goddamn clown. You

got everybody against you now. Don't pull me down with you!

EILEEN

Terry, don't talk to him like that.

> *(TERRY turns and starts to walk away. EILEEN runs after him.)*

Tee, don't! What are you doing? Don't leave me.

TERRY

You see your stupid pocketbook? I had to borrow the money to buy it. The right thing! The right thing! When I got no money, I can't always do the right thing. I can't live like you!

EILEEN

(Tries to take hold of TERRY.) Aren't you ashamed? I can't stand for you to be like this.

TERRY

Damn it, you bitch! Let go of me.

> *(Makes a gesture as if to strike her in the face. He can't. Turns away.)*

Peter, wait! I'm coming.

PETER

(Calling from extreme edge of stage.) We'll be back!

JOE

I'll be waiting.

ROSETTA

We'll be here. In our home. We'll be here!

> *(The end.)*